Decoding The Script

THE FILMMAKER'S ART

Markus Innocenti

RED DOG LOGIC

LOS ANGELES, CALIFORNIA

Book Layout & Design ©2013 — BookDesignTemplates.com
Cover Design — Red Dog Logic
Front Cover Photo from the Everett Collection, licensed through Shutterstock

Published by Red Dog Logic, an imprint of
Park Circle Limited, Glasgow, Scotland UK

ISBN 978-0-692-54976-6

FOREWORD

Most screenwriters and film directors are people you've never heard of.

The famous ones, past and present, have always been the tip of a very large iceberg. Of those who do manage to make a regular living as a key creative, most remain anonymous to all but their immediate family and colleagues. A few of us don't even try to break the surface and become 'known' — but ego being what it is, those willing to toil without caring whether they are ever recognized or not are the exception.

I'm no different from most. After 35 years in the business, I'm still trying to write, direct or produce a film that — when I mention its title — most people will go, *'Oh, yeah, I saw that'*. So far, only my music videos have that distinction — but I'm still working on it. It's been a fun journey, even if the limo rides have been few and far between.

A while back I started thinking about what I've learned in my career. You get to the point where you want to pass something on, usually because what you're seeing, and hearing, is making you slap your own forehead too many times a day.

Let me share a secret. A few days before I directed my first full-length theatrical feature film, I realized that I'd never done this before, and I wasn't sure how I was going to get through the 30-day shoot. I had no real idea how to go about making a fiction drama. I was an experienced music video director, I'd made a couple of well-received 'shorts', produced a documentary, and I'd directed some commercials. On the basis of that, the executives and the agents and the star actors figured I knew what I was doing. I was in the solitary position of knowing that when it came to direct a theatrical feature — I didn't have a clue.

Nowadays, there's so much information on filmmaking, in particular on screenwriting and directing, you begin to wonder who's buying all these books and attending all those seminars. When I started out, there was nothing except William Goldman's entertainingly brilliant *Adventures in the Screen Trade* and *Truffaut/Hitchcock* — Francois Truffaut's massive interview with Sir Alfred. Other than that, you just had to figure it out from watching other people's work and trusting that you had a 'vision'.

So how did I get to this position of having producers, agents and stars believe that my creative partner, Edward Arno, and I were ready to take the leap into making what the contract specified as a 'First Class International Theatrical Feature Film'?

I'd been an actor for a while, but when people ask how I got started I tell them I entered the film industry in a truck — which is true. I had a job delivering grip equipment from rental houses to film sets. Most deliveries were for television commercial productions, but a few were for the big features. I had an epiphany one day after I'd brought some camera support equipment to Pinewood (a major studio outside London, England). I wandered onto the *Superman* (1978) set, the movie that made Christopher Reeve famous. I couldn't get over the size of the New York street exterior set — a massive façade for the 'Daily Planet' building where 'Clark Kent' and 'Lois Lane' worked. Looking at the activity, I began to understand more fully how the magic of film was mostly smoke, mirrors and a lot of painted plywood. I guess I got fired up because within five years I co-owned a stage and film production design company and was a union-accredited Art Director.

Everything in the film business is a small-step-by-small-step progress. There are seldom instant leaps. Eight years after that day on the *Superman* set, I was a music video director. Two years after that, and I was represented by one of the big agencies and signed to co-direct my first theatrical feature. And so there I was, just a few days before Principal Photography was due to begin, nervously realizing I hadn't actually directed a major long-form dramatic work before.

Most people who are even halfway good at anything tend to forget how hard and long the journey has been and how prepared they really are when the moment of truth arrives. They often think their success has been a fluke and that at any moment someone will pull back the curtain and expose their lack of talent. I was no exception. Gripped by a full-blown case of Imposter Syndrome I began to panic — until I remembered one of the first rules of success. If you don't know — ask. Even if, in asking, you risk making yourself look ridiculous.

I called author Steven Bernstein who'd recently completed what would become the best-selling *Film Production* (a standard student text from the moment it was published by Focal Press). Steven (who was on his way to becoming one of Hollywood's A-list cinematographers and a director in his own right) took ten minutes out of his day, told me to take a deep breath, reminded me that I'd already directed thousands of set-ups, and then proceeded to give me a step-by-step method of how to walk onto a feature film set and make it look as if I knew what I was doing.

Steven Bernstein's generous insights gave me the knowledge and confidence to get through the first few hours on my debut feature without looking like a complete idiot, and since then I've built on that beginning.

Becoming a film director is no different from the learning curves and progressions made by artists working in any other of the creative arts or crafts. You start off a little unsure, a little hesitant and perhaps much too rigid in your own self-belief. Gradually, you learn how to do things the way they most often get done, you start to solve problems in ways that other artists have solved those problems before, and you feel your way towards the results you're looking for — most often with a large sense of dissatisfaction. Over time, like an improvisational jazz musician, you become so accustomed to your 'craft' and so adept at achieving your goal that you are able to apply your 'art' — the thing that distinguishes you from the others. The rules and rigidity no longer seem so necessary — but they are there to fall back on, the way a jazz musician knows the key, the mode and the scale that the musical structure relies upon.

The Filmmaker's Art series is designed to give you detailed basic knowledge that will allow you to step onto any movie set in the world and direct. From those essential basics — which every aspiring filmmaker thinks they know, but actually don't — you will establish an acceptable 'craft' and a solid jumping-off point to start creating your own 'art'.

As I go through the series, I'll be looking to take you beyond the basics so that you can develop your own signature style. Bear in mind that my goal is to take you from 'craft' to 'art' in a business where 'art' often doesn't seem to count for very much — but is completely present in the work of the masters.

Decoding The Script is the first step on a long journey, and the only book in The Filmmaker's Art series to deal with creative issues that may arise in a film's early Development Phase. The next two books in the series, *Selecting For Success* and *Shooting The List* take the concepts found in *Decoding The Script* and discuss how Directors move through Pre-Production.

If you're already on your film-making journey, or even if you've yet to begin, some of what follows may seem obvious and already acquired. I hope you'll take a moment to allow those parts which might seem familiar to soak in completely and perhaps be reassessed.

Because even the greatest musicians sit down and practice scales now and again.

A story should have a beginning, a middle, and an end... but not necessarily in that order.

—JEAN LUC GODARD

CHAPTER ONE

Interpreting The Clues

The Director is probably the only person who will ever read the script for what it is and seek to have a complete understanding of it. Producers, Actors, Cinematographers, Editors, studio Readers (script analysts) and even most Writers look at scripts in completely different ways from a Director, and — from the point of view of understanding the whole world of the film to be made — their readings are woefully incomplete.

What every person searching for a great new screenplay has in common is this; they want to find a script that they fall totally in love with. As they fall in love, they begin to see how they can add their particular skillset into the project.

It's easy to understand why nobody should fall in love with a script more fully than the Director, but the Director has to come at the script using both intuition and intellect. Passion must be tempered with cold analysis.

In short, both Heart and Head must be present as a Director reads. Facts must be gleaned. Decisions made. Ideas formed. Visions glimpsed.

- *But how does a director read a script?*

By looking for and then evaluating the following;

- Genre
- Thematic Statement
- The Story Engine
- Sub-Text
- Texture
- Image and Aural Systems

Within every screenplay you will ever read lie clues that fall under these headings. They're waiting for you to discover and evaluate. Good writers sprinkle these clues like fairy-dust throughout their work. The less-talented do not. The absence or presence of clues is, in itself, a pointer as to the worthiness and direct-ability of a script.

Decoding the Script is going to take you through this six-point checklist, give you a complete understanding of the waypoints and leave you in a position where you will never read a script the same way again, because you'll be reading like a Director.

Ready?

CHAPTER TWO

Genre

A screenplay is a blueprint that a director must decipher to make a movie. These blueprints fall into several broad categories, or 'genres'. Or should.

When you start to read a script, in fact as soon as you look at the title page, the first question uppermost in your mind should be: *'What genre is this screenplay written in?'* As your reading reveals the answer, your next questions must be: *'Does this genre interest me?'* and *'Can I work within this genre in an effective and original way?'*

The problem is that many of the most interesting scripts mix and match genres, and the genres themselves seem to be myriad and to have all kinds of sub-genres within them. So, the first problem is correctly identifying which genre the screenplay falls into.

If you were to take a quick look at a list of films in a single genre — I'm going to use Sci-Fi as my example of a "broad" genre — you might start to see the problems you'll be dealing with.

Sci-Fi can include such wildly different films as Alex Proyas' *Dark City* (New Line, 1998), Stanley Kubrick's *2001: A Space Odyssey* (MGM, 1968), Barry Sonnenfeld's *Men In Black* (Columbia Pictures, 1997), Andrei Tarkovsky's *Solaris* (Mosfilm, 1972), Ridley Scott's *Blade Runner* (Warner Bros, 1982), Joseph Kosinski's *Oblivion* (Universal Pictures, 2013), and Alex Garland's *Ex Machina* (Universal Pictures, 2015) — oh, yeah and Christopher Ray's *Mega Shark vs. Crocosaurus* (The Asylum, 2010).

A list of quality Sci-Fi films could go on endlessly but it's sufficient to show the vast differences within a single genre and how you need a way to sub-categorize. *Dark City* might be Sci-Fi/Psychological Thriller. *Men In Black* might be Sci-Fi/Comedy. *Blade Runner* is usually considered Sci-Fi/Thriller. *Solaris* always seems to be listed as purely 'Sci-Fi' but you might want to add a sub-category like 'Psychological Drama' because that seems to be the primary interest for director Tarkovsky in his handling of the story. In Steven Soderbergh's remake (20th Century Fox, 2002) the sub-genre becomes more 'Romance' and 'Mystery' orientated.

These combo platters of genre hold true for films in all the primary genres. You might think 'Horror' is pretty well defined — but is it? Wes Craven's *The Last House On The Left* (Hallmark Releasing, 1972) is 'Horror', but has so many elements of the 'Crime' genre it cannot be categorized in the same way as, say, Dario Argento's *Suspiria* (International Classic, 1977) which, with it's 'Occult' element, has more in common with Roman Polanski's *Rosemary's Baby* (Paramount, 1968).

Nobody can agree on anything.

I've seen David Fincher's *Se7en* (New Line, 1995) described as belonging to the 'Horror' genre. Clearly, it's a 'Mystery Crime Thriller', but it has 'Horror' elements. Saul Dibb's *The*

Duchess (Paramount Vantage, 2008) is 'Historical Drama', but could equally well fall under the 'Romance' category. You've seen Rob Reiner's *When Harry Met Sally* (Castle Rock, 1989) and you might think it's less of a 'Comedy' and more of a 'Romance'. Many people think of it as a 'Romantic Comedy'. However, unlike the average run-of-the-mill 'Rom-Com' you could almost make the argument that its exploration of relationships and commitment makes it a 'Social Drama'.

Like I say. Nobody can agree on anything. As a Director you have to at least be able to agree with yourself and promote your point-of-view.

The reality is that most of the mainstream movies you see in multiplexes combine genres. Here's a list of the genre-mix for the top ten grossing pictures in theaters this weekend. No titles necessary.

- Action Adventure Sci-Fi Thriller
- Action Adventure Sci-Fi
- Action Comedy
- Action Crime Thriller
- Action Comedy
- Drama Romance
- Animation Family Adventure Comedy
- Drama Sci-Fi
- Drama
- Comedy Music

Interesting list. 10% Animation - that sometimes goes as high as 30% depending on the time of year. 50% are primarily Action movies. 30% of these titles utilize Comedy genre elements. 10% Family. 10% Crime. 10% Music. 10% Romance. Actually, it's 20% 'Romance' because the title at #9 which thinks it's a single genre — 'Drama' — is actually a 'Historical Romance' derived from a 'Famous 19th Century Novel' — which is pretty much a sub-genre of its own. 100% in multi-genre formats. It's been this way for years.

Curious, I delved further to see what the genre spread for this Memorial Day weekend looks like in my zip code. Of the sixty movies being screened, all are multi-genre with the exception of four, one being 'Horror' and three 'Drama'.

On closer inspection, the 'Horror' is also 'Supernatural' and the 'Drama' trio are respectively 'Romance', 'Addiction' and the 'Historical Romance' mentioned previously. There are five Documentaries screening — but these too can all be sub-genred into 'Nature', 'Sports', 'Biography', 'Travel' and 'Music'. That's a lot of Docs making it onto the big screen on a holiday weekend. Surprisingly.

Take out the 5 Docs, and the 55 multi-genre movies screening this holiday weekend break down into their sub-genres as follows;

Action	10
Adventure	9
Animation	3
Comedy	20
Crime	6
Drama	18
Fantasy	3
Family	5
Horror	3
Musical	4
Mystery	4
Romance	5
Sci-Fi	4
Thriller	10
War	1
Western	1

The reason why this pedantic recitation should interest you will become apparent shortly. We are, of course, analyzing the genre-mix of films that have attained the Holy Grail of a theatrical release and are, almost without exception, movies released by the major studios.

It is often suggested that in the world of independent, lower budget production, combining genres is risky. In *How To Make Money Making Movies: The Secrets of Becoming a Profitable Filmmaker* (Wbusiness Books, 2009), Tanya York and co-author Randall Frakes make the point that mixing genres risks missing the target audience.

It's a good point, not just because the audience that makes Low-Budget (or Micro-Budget) films profitable is quite single-minded in taste and expectation — but also because it's easier to leave no doubt in a distributor's mind about what kind of film is being offered. To combine genres in the way that big studio movies so often do can make a film a difficult sell at lower budget levels where immediacy and simplicity is the principal requirement.

Beginning to see where I'm taking you? If you've already passed the stage of having your first movie out there in distribution — let's say it was a horror movie about carnivorous spiders made on a budget of $100,000 — then good for you. Unless you want to continue in the same way, you need to move onwards and upwards and start reading scripts that mix genres. You might also be astute enough to realize that a script with either 'War' or 'Western' as one of its sub-genre elements might be a tough sell for theatrical distribution and that having 'Action' and 'Comedy' in your genre description might be a safer bet.

Equally, if you've yet to make your first movie —and, assuming you're neither the scion of an entertainment dynasty nor an internationally-known actor — then you probably want to find a script that can be made 'low budget' and is firmly in a single genre. Horror. Comedy. Drama.

- *Okay, Mr. Innocenti. That's Business. How about 'Art'?*

All we need to know is this simple rule;

- *Emerging Directors must be aware of which genres they will work best in.*

A Clue lies in the kind of movies that you are most drawn to. If you hate Music and Animation, chances are you'll make a poor director in those genres, or you'll be miserable making pictures you're not interested in —should you even get a chance to do so. If Horror revolts you, it's unlikely you'll be able to add anything to the genre. If, on the other hand, Horror fascinates and darkly amuses you — you might become a highly original horror director quicker than we can say 'Mario Bava'.

Passion gets noticed in Hollywood. It's the bright-burning fuel that helps you make your way in the business. Let's imagine that 'Horror' is your primary genre. It's all you talk about — as your ex-lovers will probably attest. You live it, breathe it, dream it. It's a good bet that every time you go into a meeting with the Suits you'll know more about the genre than anyone else in the room. (But, trust me, the Suits will know a surprising amount so be careful not to underestimate them).

Your passion and genre knowledge will impress the Executives, the Money and the Star Talent and will carry you into production, where — if you remain lucky —you'll be surrounded by collaborators who share your passion. You need to be the person who knows the genre backwards. Better than anyone else on the set.

While there's plenty of 'upside' to being an expert in a particular 'genre' or 'genres', the 'downside' is if you want to shift your career from your chosen 'genre' to something completely different — like a shift from 'Horror' to 'Romantic Comedy' — well, good luck with that. Probably the only way to do it is to make so much money in your 'genre' that you cannot be denied a 'labor of love' project. And that movie better be astonishing. So, no pressure there!

But we're getting ahead of ourselves.

You might be thinking that all this talk of 'genre', and its importance in so many aspects of your career, is limiting your creativity. After all, there are numerous examples of directors who have excelled in many different genres. If you love and have a deep understanding of movies of all types, it's reasonable to suppose that you could excel in several 'genres'.

This might be true. But before you get the opportunity to find out which ones those are, you're going to get judged. So, please keep this rule in mind;

- *Be Careful Before You Commit To A Script*

This point is made very, very seriously. It's hard to get a picture to direct. When the opportunity arrives, most of us will accept what we're given just for that golden chance to become a director. So, I say it again;

- *Be Careful Before You Commit To A Script*

Think very carefully about the material. If it doesn't truly appeal to you, be honest with yourself. It's hard to say 'no' but it might be the smartest thing you'll ever do. It is far, far better to wait another year, if need be, for the project that is right for you than to waste a year making a film that doesn't wrap itself around your heart and cling on.

The first film you make will define you as a filmmaker. Perhaps not forever, but maybe for a long, long time. Nothing is more frustrating that being known as *'the guy who did that weird stoner comedy'* when your passion is to make serious, tragic films about moral redemption. Every meeting you take (and they will dwindle to nothing over the years if you make the mistake of choosing wrong early in your career) will be marked by confusion and disappointment.

Nothing kills careers quicker than meeting with executives who think you're one thing and then find out from you that their perception is wrong. In Hollywood, powerbrokers hate to find that their assumptions are incorrect. You've been labeled before you walk in the door. If the label doesn't fit — take a hike. We specialize in this world — until we get powerful enough to change our course.

This is why decoding the first clue in the script is so important in several ways. This is your career. What kind of career do you want? What passion and knowledge do you bring to the table? Can the 'genre' you're working in sustain your enthusiasm, excitement and interest not just for a day or two — but for months on end. Years, maybe. Are you so in touch with the 'genre' of the screenplay you've been given that you can steer it the way it needs to go? Can you safely take it out of the screenwriter's hands and throw it up on a screen so well and so completely that an audience of 'genre-philes' will nod their heads in awed acknowledgement of what you've done?

You've been handed a script — or opened the PDF that landed in your Dropbox — and it's exciting. Someone thinks you might be worth attaching as Director of their project. That's flattering — but you've got to put the feeling aside and do some serious reading. Some decoding.

The title page is your first opportunity to determine genre. *American Sniper* is fairly obvious. *The Age of Adaline* less so. By page three of any screenplay you're considering, the genre should be clear. (Occasionally, a screenplay will start in one genre and turn into another — but seldom successfully).

See how far you can get before you discover the genre of the screenplay. If it takes more than four pages, then the script is a candidate for the trashcan.

Once you have identified the genre, you need to ask yourself this important question;

- *Is this script in a genre, or a genre-mix, that I can truly excel in?*

If not, then send the script back with a polite *'Pass'*. But, if the answer is 'yes', then keep reading because there's a number of other questions to answer before you can give yourself the 'green light' to direct the script, and a whole bunch of further decoding work to complete — all of which will enable you to direct the script properly.

CHAPTER THREE

Thematic Statement

Francis Coppola makes singularly expressive films using a technique that allows him to hold together the core of the film throughout its entire creation. Mr. Coppola's trick is to find a single word that expresses everything about the story. He strives, with each project, to encapsulate the theme so completely in one word that it's impossible to let it go. The word becomes a talisman, a touchstone that allows him to filter all decisions, deflect all conflicting paths and channel all creativity into a story that will express and reveal that word.

That works for Francis Coppola. Mere mortals, such as your humble author, require a little embellishment — but the trick remains the same.

- *You need to be able to state the Theme of the movie you are going to make in a single sentence*

If it works for you to do so in one word, then go for it — but it is essential to have a Thematic Statement and it must lie there in the script for you to discover and reveal. If you cannot develop a Thematic Statement from your reading of the script then one of two things should happen. Either, the script should land in the trashcan — or you should reconsider your readiness to become a director.

Nobody else involved with the project will come up with a (Director's) Thematic Statement. The writer, if any good, might have one (although writers generally have something less robust). In short, having a Thematic Statement separates you from everyone else who reads the script.

Moreover, the ease or difficulty you have in being able to craft a Thematic Statement is a good guide to how well-written the script is, and how clearly you have an understanding of what you've read.

A rule of thumb is; the earlier in your reading of the script that you can formulate your single sentence, the stronger the script is going to be and the deeper will be your understanding.

How do you state a theme? First, let me explain what it is not.

- *It's not a tag line or a log line*

A tag line (a.k.a. 'catch-line') is a marketing device. The one everyone remembers is for Ridley Scott's *Alien* (20th Century Fox, 1979);

In Space Nobody Can Hear You Scream

A properly conceived tag line points to genre and basic storyline. With the *Alien* example, the audience is being told that this is a film with Sci-Fi and Horror elements.

A log line is something you'd find in TV Guide or an online movie description and goes like this;

Hunted for a murder he didn't commit, Joe hides out in a quiet, mid West town, where he meets and marries Helen, the local postmistress.

Neither Tag line nor Log line are anything close to a (Director's) Thematic Statement. What we directors are talking about is the exposition, in a single sentence, of the guts of the story.

Theme — to use a dictionary definition — is the unifying, dominant idea in a work of art, or in just about anything that springs from the imagination into something that we can all become aware of.

In restaurant design, it's generally obvious — we walk into the establishment and there it is. A sushi restaurant's dominant 'theme' tends not to evoke the ambiance of a Texan BBQ joint. In writing, the dominant idea is harder to discern — but dig beneath the surface and you will gradually find the principal, underlying concern that lies at the heart of the tale.

Theme is the 'core' of the story. Everything else orbits around it. That doesn't mean that the writer sat down and said to herself; *'Oh, I just came up with a great Theme for my new screenplay'*. More often, a writer has a 'Concept' or a 'Premise'— the initial story idea, the spark — which, as they develop the idea, consciously or (sometimes) unconsciously, suggests a Theme. Once the Theme becomes apparent, good writers, self-aware writers, set out to "prove" it.

You could be forgiven for thinking that 'Theme', 'Idea', 'Concept' and 'Premise' are words that mean much the same thing. Some writers think those words *do* mean the same thing — but they don't — and making that mistake results in indifferent, one-dimensional writing. One of your primary tasks, as a Film Director, is to differentiate between good screenplays and bad, and identifying the Theme — or lack of it — is a vital part of that.

But although we may now understand that 'Theme' isn't a 'tag line' or a 'log line', the bad news is that it often gets confused with other buzz words.

When writers go to pitch meetings with the Suits, they are seldom asked; *'What's the theme of your screenplay?'*. Instead, they are asked, *'What's the concept?'* or *'Give me the premise.'* The Writer then dutifully gives an 'elevator pitch'.

What happens is the Writer lays out — in the fewest sentences possible — the 'Concept', the 'story idea' that sparked a flame big enough to turn into 90-plus pages. To give you a 'Concept' example, I could have the 'story idea' or 'premise' that a suicidal cop takes huge risks because he doesn't care if he lives or dies, and in doing so successfully tackles crime. That's a 'Concept'. You probably recognize the picture if you can recall Mel Gibson and Danny Glover's on-screen partnership.

'Theme' steps deeper into the story than 'concept', 'premise' or 'story idea'. Theme is a glimpse, and in the best writing it's a very powerful glimpse, of what lies underneath the story. It reveals the humanity beneath the 'concept'. It identifies the values, experiences and emotions that play on the characters and shape the circumstances they find themselves in.

For this reason, a Theme deals with big issues. Love, Hatred, Loss, Loneliness, Redemption, Sacrifice, Success, Isolation. You can begin to see where Francis Coppola gets his 'Word'.

You may also see how good thematic writing, which introduces the big issues, deepens a screenplay. Audiences respond to that. A story about a suicidal cop which merely played on one dimension and didn't explore that character's loneliness and alienation, his experience of loss, the whole gamut of his emotional life — would be a story that would wither and fade. Leaving audiences unengaged.

This is why, once you've done the relatively easy work of decoding the genre you're dealing with, you should next try to discern the Theme. As you read the screenplay, try to make sense of it in a thoughtful sentence that might sum it up. That sentence could be similar to these; *'Simplicity of character results in Fame, Fortune and Lasting Love'* or *'The Search for Identity brings Hardship but leads to Happiness'* or *'Taking Revenge leads to Unbearable Loss'*. Notice I capitalize the Big Issue words in each sentence. Francis Coppola might have chosen *'Simplicity'*, *'Identity'* and *'Revenge'* in each case.

Clearly, you might be wrong. You could come up with an interesting Thematic Statement by page ten, but by page thirty the script might have developed in an unexpected way. No problem. Just re-align your Statement. However, by mid-point in the script, you should have a clear Thematic Statement — the theme should have presented itself to you, and the script should continue to move towards a conclusion that will fully express that theme.

An alternative way to get to your Thematic Statement is not, perhaps, to focus on the Big Issues — but to find a Statement that reflects either the mindscape of the leading character(s) or, more powerfully, the understanding you want the audience to have and to feel. To give you an example, Nicolas Roeg's thriller *Don't Look Now* (British Lion, 1973) could be described as a gothic horror meditation on Death. Roeg's Thematic Statement, according to reliable sources, was *'We Are Not Prepared'*. Everything — everything — that occurs in this film is unexpected, both for the leading characters and the audience. From the drowning that is the 'Ignition Event', to the controversial sex scene between Donald Sutherland and Julie Christie's characters. From Julie Christie's fainting spell in the restaurant, to Sutherland's accident in the church.

Technically, this Thematic Statement is carried through as well. The cinematography shows a Venice that is entirely unexpected — a city empty of tourists. The editing is constantly jarring and unorthodox, images thrown at us that we do not *expect*. The Act III "reveal" of the character in the red coat is the single most obvious thing that we — as an audience — are not prepared for. Finally, the terrible realization of Donald Sutherland's character that forms the ending of the film is something that he —and we — have had no preparation for. Mr. Roeg followed his Thematic Statement completely and *proved it* so well that the film sits comfortably in many 'Best Lists' and continues to draw admirers.

- *So, what's your point?*

Most good, and all great, directors identify, interpret and demonstrate the Theme. Then, like the skilled writer, they set out to "prove" it.

- *Prove it?*

Well, yes.

Let's use the example of the Thematic Statement; '*Taking Revenge leads to Unbearable Loss*'. If you direct the film in such a way that the Revenge results in a Loss that is pretty tough but not Unbearable, you haven't proved the Thematic Statement and you've weakened the script rather than enhanced it.

Equally, if you read a script that appears by mid-point to have the '*Taking Revenge leads to Unbearable Loss*' theme — and it turns out by the last page that the person taking revenge loses a girlfriend he doesn't really care for, along with a couple of tickets to the ballgame — then the script has failed to "prove" the theme it appeared to be offering. The screenplay offered a story with a poor 'result'.

This is why, as a director, you should be trying to formulate your Thematic Statement from the first page. How fast can you identify the Thematic Statement in the screenplay you've been handed? How well does the writer bring it out, hint at it in the first sentences even, and then set out to prove it?

Formulating your Thematic Statement performs another benefit. It informs your reading of the script, gives you a 'zoomed-out' view of the screenplay and helps you see how the sequences progress towards the story's 'result'. If the script fails to march towards the 'result' with the structure hinted at in the Thematic Statement you've formulated, then the chances are it's a story that is not well told and it's time to raise a mental red flag.

'Taking Revenge leads to Unbearable Loss' is a Thematic Statement which suggests that in Act I something happens that requires, in the protagonist's mind, the taking of Revenge. The end of Act 1 might climax in the decision to act, or in the Revenge itself. Act II would then follow the conflicts and troubles resulting from that decision, with Act III bringing the Unbearable Loss. The path of the protagonist and the story itself is revealed in your Thematic Statement.

You'll notice I've been using the word 'result' instead of 'resolution'. Everyone seems to think that stories need to be 'resolved'. It ain't necessarily so. I can think of many wonderful movies where there is no 'resolution', but the 'result' is plain. Also, 'resolve' isn't as active a word as 'result' — and we need to stay active if we're going to direct.

But I don't want you to think that the 'result' you're looking for means that the characters have to change. Many people feel, and they're mostly actors and studio readers, that a character must have an 'arc'. Not so. Lajos Egri, probably the greatest of all the writing gurus, pointed out that character has to be rich and deep, and not just a puppet of the plot. But being rich and deep doesn't mean that the character has to be 'changed' in the course of the story. 'Indiana Jones' does not change. 'James Bond' does not change (well, only with glacier-like pace to keep in tune with the socio-political times).

It'd be a sad cinema universe without the 'Stranger' archetype — the previously unknown individual who arrives on the scene and changes the lives of everyone else in the story but who, himself, is unchanged. Clearly, you have to stay alert to the 'rules' of a particular genre and how the characters behave — but don't dismiss a good story because one or more of the characters doesn't have the so-called 'arc'.

There are people who think that the natural evolution of the story shouldn't be interfered with, that writers needn't hold a Theme in mind if there's a strong 'concept'. I have to disagree. We're artists. We must stay ahead of our audience. The writer has to know where she is going from page one, and directors have to be able to smell the coffee and know that the aroma is indeed 'coffee'. If writer and director are unsure of what they are laying out and seeking to prove, then a meandering script will result in a movie that has no back-bone and which doesn't know the *direction* it's going in.

CHAPTER FOUR

It's Your Call

Within the first few pages, you should have established Genre and a *possible* Thematic Statement. You might have decided the screenplay appeals to you, but now you have to decide if the script is any good. No point working on a script with an appealing Genre and the suggestion of a powerful Thematic Statement if, in all other respects, it's a total waste of your time and skills.

Whether the script is any good or not is *entirely* your call. As I mentioned earlier, you are the only person who will ever look at the script and determine its overall quality. Nobody else has the faintest idea (which is one of the many reasons bad movies are made).

The script reader who did the 'coverage' and told the producer to consider buying the script did the job in terms of literary and film production quality and marketability. He looked at the 'concept' or 'premise', the structure, the pace, the dialogue, the uniqueness of setting, the potential for specific casting, perhaps even the possibility of co-production, distribution and funding opportunities. He didn't make any decision about the quality of the script from the director's point of view — because he didn't know.

With the option acquired, the producer will be talking up the script like it's The Second Coming because it cost her money. Besides, if it doesn't feel right, or someone higher on the food chain has a doubt, then she'll hire a rewrite team to make it "better".

I could be facetious and say that the actors only read *their* parts and that, when they receive a script, their role has already been highlighted to make it easier for them to find their dialogue. This, of course, would be completely untrue.

Everyone else tends to look at the script to find out how their department is going to deal with the issues involved. They may feel privately that the script isn't quite right — but it isn't their job to voice an opinion about matters that don't fall under their department.

What you will *never* hear is this innocent little question;

- *Does anybody know if this script is any good?*

The question doesn't get asked, because that's a dangerously challenging question which could have unforeseen repercussions if anyone got tempted to respond. As William Goldman so succinctly reminded us; this is Hollywood — nobody knows anything.

It's up to you — the director — to find out if this script is any good and can be translated from the pages to the screen.

This is your job — and only your job. *But how?*

CHAPTER FIVE

The Story Engine

A script is a vehicle. To make a movie, you put a star in the vehicle. The director gets behind the wheel and points it where he wants to go. The audience comes along for the ride.

The story is the engine that keeps your vehicle in motion on its wild journey in the dark.

Scripts only work if they have stories. In *The Typewriter, The Rifle and The Movie Camera* (BFI, 1996) Adam Simon's documentary film about legendary director Sam Fuller, Tim Robbins asks the cigar-toting Godfather of Indie filmmaking; "What makes a good film?" Sam growls back; "A story." Robbins persists; "What makes a good story?" Sam grins; "*A story!*"

- *Too many films don't have stories, let alone good ones.*

There's a forest of books available about screenwriting and the analysis of story and structure. Invariably, these are targeted towards screenwriters. The authors are too numerous to list, and some have expressed the essential principles better than others. A few have written books that have become 'scripture' and caused reams of dogmatic and formulaic screenplays to hit slush piles near you. There are producers, agents, story editors, casting directors, actors, screenwriters, financiers and lawyers who have developed extremely fixed ideas on what makes a good screenplay, entirely based on their readings of a number of well-intentioned and intelligently presented books.

But like so many good intentions, the work of several authors has been misinterpreted, over-analyzed or over-simplified by people eager to grasp the Truth.

- *And the truth is, none of these books were written for directors.*

So, I have to present to you — in the hope that nothing I mention becomes dogma — a method of seeing the components in the Story Engine purely from a Director's point-of-view.

Some of the terms I am going to use have their parallels in elements identified by authors of screenwriting books. For example, many of us are familiar with an important script element called the 'Inciting Incident'. I'm writing about a Story Engine, so my term for that element is the 'Ignition Event'.

The screenplay is the power plant of the film you are going to make. The Engine is effective and responsive because of the use of Gears and the Driver's (Director's) pressure on the gas pedal and the brakes.

A journey in which a vehicle moves using only one gear, and with a constant single pressure on the gas pedal, is a boring journey indeed. The engine is a monotonous moan. There are scripts like that.

A vehicle which moves in fits and starts — jerking forwards one minute then stalling, speeding headlong another, making a quick stop and a reverse for no good reason — there are scripts like that too.

- *Stories only work if the Pistons in the Story Engine are moving — and moving in opposition.*

What do I mean by that?

Simply that a good story must have constant movement and a structure in which the events being described are shifting in as dramatic a way as a piston being either "up" or "down" in an engine's cylinder.

This sounds convoluted, and it's something that I didn't "get" myself until a year or so before I became a director. What gave me an instant understanding was Steven Spielberg's *Indiana Jones and the Raiders of The Lost Ark* (Paramount, 1981).

For me, watching *Raiders* was like looking at one of those 'exploded' views of an engine you see in auto magazines or the 'cutaway' diagrams of human anatomy you sometimes see in medical offices.

Raiders is a classic learning text as far as I'm concerned — largely because none of it is subtle. The Engine is huge, and the internal movement is in your face. Think about that opening sequence — a sequence the whole world knows. To paraphrase it considerably: Indy escapes horrible death to get to the primitive altar. Indy gets the treasure. Indy gets chased by a big stone ball. Indy survives and lands in a heap outside the cave. Indy finds himself surrounded by savage Indians and the malicious Frenchman. Indy escapes. Indy gets chased. Indy gets on the biplane. Indy finds a snake in the cockpit…

What is happening here, and the thing that makes this film so satisfying and watchable, is this constant movement — the backward and forward shift from Indy with a big smile of relief on his face, to Indy getting into another problem from which there seems no escape.

For the sake of our understanding as Directors, the entire Sequence has the Pistons moving the story forward in intriguing and unexpected ways. The Pistons are either up or down, moving that story engine forward quickly or slowing down when the director takes his foot off the gas while an obstacle or unexpected event is anticipated or negotiated. In a satisfying story, there should be no mistaking the fact that the Engine is working and that a constant oppositional movement is taking place.

1. PISTON MOVEMENT

When you're reading a script with a view to directing it, you have to examine each scene to see if the Pistons are moving. Does the scene have movement? I don't mean 'motion' — I mean is there an event or events in the scene that moves the situation from one position to another? Does the scene start at the "top" and go to the "bottom"? Does something happen in the scene that takes us from "Red" to "Green"? Are the Pistons moving in true opposition? Because if they are not, we have to check why the scene is there at all.

I say "check" because this idea of 'piston movement' isn't dogma. It isn't a rule that *must* occur. Not all scenes have to start in one position and end up elsewhere. A scene can be neutral, balancing on the edge of going in one direction or another. A scene can be present to provide exposition, mood, anticipation, punctuation or even breathing space. We all know the Establishing Shot — and that's invariably a scene without a Piston Movement.

That said, an overall lack of Piston Movement in a script points to poor storytelling. It's hard to direct a good picture from a bad story, but that's the job we're often called upon to do — and one of the tricks to making it better is to introduce some oppositional movement into your scenes.

For now, you might find it useful, as you read the script you've been offered, to color highlight the Sluglines of scenes that have good Piston Movement, then use a different color for scenes that don't, and yet another for scenes that are 'neutral'. Flick through the entire script at the end of your reading and see which color predominates.

Since *Raiders*, many films have been made that seek to emulate the breathless and unforgettable thrill-ride that Steven Spielberg and George Lucas took us on. Billions of dollars have been spent on movies that have not remained in the hearts and minds of the audience for longer than their opening weekend. These movies all had one thing in common. Huge, gigantic, super-colossal Piston Movement. But every single one of those super-expensive fiascos failed for one simple, foreseeable reason. They all lacked an important, easily identifiable Story Engine Component.

- *And that would be?*

2. THE GEAR SHIFT

Whenever something happens to shift a character's original expectation, belief or viewpoint — that's a Gear Shift. It's similar to a Piston Movement, but it's something that a Director looks to be expressed in human terms, by an Actor.

Let me clarify the Gear Shift and separate it from the Piston Movement.

If, in the summer blockbuster you are probably waiting to see on Blu-Ray, the Super-Hero flings the Super-Villain through a building — that's a Piston Movement. When, in retaliation, the Super-Villain tosses the Super-Hero into a blazing oil tanker — that's another Piston Movement. Most blockbusters are content with that — great excitement is supposedly being generated. Some of us may feel it's as interesting as watching a 2-hour Ping-Pong game with very loud sound effects, but we can all agree the Engine is working hard and we can admire the shiny Pistons in motion.

However, suppose there was a line in the script which (gasp) resulted in a shot being put into the movie indicating that the Super-Hero has a moment of realization. A realization that he's not as weak as he thinks he is, and he can take down the Super-Villain if he just tries harder. That's a Gear Shift. Similarly, if the Super-Villain crushes the Super-Hero with the Empire State Building and the triumphant snarl on his face turns to dismay as the Super-Hero emerges from the rubble dusting down his spandex — that's another Gear Shift.

Empire State Building crushing Super-Hero — Piston Movement. Super-Villain realizing he's going to get super-ass kicked. Gear Shift.

Indiana Jones, as we've mentioned, undergoes tremendous and almost violent Gear Shifts, while all around him the Pistons scream in motion. Gear shifting from Relief to Fright. From Amusement to Revulsion.

This is what we love about storytelling. Yes, we get a thrill from the Pistons working to drive us forward through the story — but we empathize with the character undergoing Gear Shifts. The love and bonding we experience with so many world-famous characters is due to observing them as they Gear Shift. It's this humanity that many of the mega-movies either don't take time to develop, or ignore completely, because the character is too awesome to respond to a situation with a human Gear Shift.

Now, a Gear Shift doesn't have to be some kind of polar opposite, nor does it have to be dramatically over the top to remain interesting and engaging.

If you take a simple everyday example, you'll see that Gear Shifts occur to every one of us, all the time...

You get up one morning, looking forward to your first day off in a month, and, while you're sitting at Starbucks planning a lazy day ahead, your boss calls to say there's an

emergency and you're needed. The Piston moved, and —
judging by the expression on your face —you just went through
a Gear Shift.

Creating those Gear Shifts, while keeping the Pistons
moving, is the mark of a good screenwriter — and the mark of
a good director is being able to execute what the writer has
laid out. I guarantee that favorite scenes in your favorite movies
have a Gear Shift or two within them. Here's a favorite scene of
mine;

In Rainer W. Fassbinder's *Ali: Fear Eats The Soul* (New
Yorker Films, 1975), an elderly widow discovers her family are
horrified that she has fallen in love with a young African immigrant. She goes from Happiness to Despair in a single brilliant
scene, while her upright and loving family is revealed as con-
temptible, racist and hate-filled — thus making their own Gear
Shift. And yes, the Gear Shifts in this particular scene — many
of them extremely subtle —resulted in a Piston Movement
which propelled the story into its next stage. What was the Piston Movement? The elderly lady (played so wonderfully by
Brigitte Mira), has her expectation of a happy family life, and
marriage to the man she loves, completely over-turned. Green
to Red. Hot to Cold. But accomplished through subtle, and
sometimes not so subtle, Gear Shifting from the entire cast.

Many Gear Shifts are easy to identify because they ob-
servably go from one extreme to another. Hopeful to Hopeless.
Possibility to Impossibility. Bravado to Cowardice. Fear to
Fearlessness. Aggression to Conciliation. This is why a Gear
Shift tends to get confused with a Piston Movement. When
these large Gear Shifts occur, it does feel that the scene has
gone from "top" to "bottom" or from "Red" to "Green". It's
tempting to regard these as Piston Movements — but they're
not. If something gets 'shifted' due to a human reaction — it's
a Gear Shift. All those fond of marking scripts with highlighter
— choose a 'Gear Shift' color and mark the moment when it
occurs.

Gear Shifts produce Piston Movement, of course, because the Engine is running — but the audience is unaware of the Piston movement because their attention has been drawn to the Gear Shift. It's this mechanical effect that makes a film move forward seamlessly and contributes to a continuity of motion within the story.

Here's a Gear Shift that is under-played. Beautifully. It's from James Ivory's *The Remains Of The Day* (Columbia, 1993). I'm going to talk about this film in further volumes of *The Filmmaker's Art*, so I hope you'll take a couple of hours to view it if you haven't seen it already.

In the scene known as "Brightening His Room", Emma Thompson's character 'Miss Kenton', a housekeeper in a stately English manor house, brings the butler, 'Mr. Stevens' (Anthony Hopkins), some flowers to brighten his private living space — and to show that she is interested in him and wants to provide a feminine element in his life. 'Miss Kenton' expects that this small demonstration of gentleness, intimacy and affection will bring 'Mr. Stevens' out of his shell and begin a warmer relationship. However, 'Mr. Stevens' is so uncomfortable with intimacy he finds a way to scold 'Miss Kenton' for being unprofessional. Emma Thompson *subtly shifts* from Warm Affection to Cold and Silent Fury. The scene becomes the springboard that the rest of the movie works from. It's a dramatic and important shift for 'Miss Kenton' at a vital point in the story line, and the director had to be fully aware of not only how this ought to be played, but also that this particular Gear Shift — while minor in it's subtle, delicately judged performance — initiates a major Piston movement that signals the end of Act 1 and propels the audience into Act II of the movie.

If a script doesn't have these shifts of character viewpoint and understanding, these constantly changing and very human Gear Shifts, then you'll have a fundamental writing problem — and if it's not fixed it'll become a fundamental directing problem. The Gear Shifts, you see, give you something to direct. You're watching and deciding if the Actor is going too hard in the Gear Shift, or not revealing it enough. This goes a long way to explain John Huston's directorial style. Huston collaborated with some of the best actors of his day, legends like Robert Mitchum and Ingrid Bergman. His direction was to say things like *'Just a little more, Ingrid'* or *'Take it down a bit, Bob'*.

Huston was watching how the Actors performed the Gear Shift present in the script and then he applied the Gas Pedal or the Brake just enough to help them get it right. He used to say that directing was 50% casting correctly. He was right. And a good portion of the rest is helping the Actor negotiate the Gear Shift.

3. THE IGNITION EVENT

To conclude our vehicle analogy, and thank you for putting up with it, the most beautifully designed and built automobile in the world is worthless until you have 'engine ignition' by pressing the start button. Scripts, and the movies made from them, are no different. They are useless without the ignition that gets the story moving.

This 'Ignition Event' or 'Inciting Incident' turns out to be one of the things that people who are not directors — but who are film professionals of one stripe or another — get very anxious about. In this instance, they have some reason.

The dogma is that if there isn't an onscreen incident, important event or discovery *within the First Ten Pages* then the screenplay should proceed immediately to the dumpster — or the rewrite room.

Ideally, you do want to find something in those First Ten Pages that 'ignites' the story and sets the principal characters in *motion*. The problem is that formulaic 'dogma' has caused many writers to spark their stories with high-explosives when a gently-struck match would do the job. The concern over audience attention (or lack of) means that movies tend to begin with a huge bang that seeks to grab the audience, and which gives an implied promise that once grabbed, the movie won't let go.

I'm not suggesting that the Ignition Event isn't needed — clearly it is to get the vehicle moving — but just be careful that it's well-judged in its size. An Ignition Event can be subtle — and it can even "happen" before the screenplay begins. Properly written, the Ignition is the story embryo. If it feels like something that got slapped onto the script in a cloning experiment that went badly wrong — then it's wrong. The Ignition has to feel that it is the true seed of the story — the essential origin of it. To be truly successful it should have an element of 'foreshadowing' and that long shadow should ultimately fall across the lives of all the characters.

The 'Ignition' is your starting point. Some Ignition Sequences are massive, overblown and disproportionate. Others are subtler, and frequently tend towards vagueness — those movies where you're not quite sure what is happening or why, but the action you're puzzling over is later revealed to have been the 'Ignition'.

Every storyteller who has ever lived will tell you that you need to 'open' in such a way that attention is focused, and the audience engaged. It's up to you to first find the 'Ignition', determine if it is placed in a way that gives the story the propulsion it needs, and figure out — and this is the difficult part — just how big an explosion you need to get the Pistons moving in the vehicle you're driving.

The absolute bottom line on 'Ignition'?

Don't make a film without one.

CHAPTER SIX

The First Ten

Most good distributors, producers and directors will know by Page Ten if they have a quality script in their hands or not. This is because a well-written producible script will have six common elements. You'll be pleased to learn that we've discussed four of them already — but here are the other two to round off your "First Ten" analytical skills.

1. THE SPECIAL WORLD

Very early on in the script you are reading (no later than Page Ten), the screenplay should present a 'Special World' that will only ever exist in the film you make.

Naturally, the Writer may describe a world that is clearly present, visible and "real" — but ideally it should portray a place, a time or a situation most of us have not entered before. A penitentiary in Illinois, a courtroom in Los Angeles, a Greenwich Village apartment in the 1960's, a nuclear submarine under the ice-cap, a Grand Hotel with a notorious past, a Cuban nightclub famous from a previous decade, a lumber yard in Oregon, a roadside diner in the South-West, a television station on the East Coast, a casino in Nevada, a theme-park on an island 500 miles west of Hawaii, a farm in Idaho, an immigrant ghetto outside Paris.

Do you notice what's happening here?

The settings may be commonplace, or they may be exotic — it doesn't matter. What matters is they're specific and 'Special'. Your film will define and make them more specific still — but unless there's a 'Special World' presented in the screenplay, there is no story and you aren't transporting your audience anywhere.

Film academics call this *diagesis* and talk about a movie's *diagetic world* — meaning the elements of the internal world created by the story. Just in case you wondered.

Here's an interesting thing. When you're in production, the 'Special World' will assert itself. If you haven't expected it, then it will feel like a strange and wonderful thing. It may take a day or two, but the 'world' of the film will suddenly wrap itself around you. It will be as if you'd stepped into a space that only exists in the film you are making. A bubble that contains all the locations, all the characters, all the possibilities — and nothing else. If something intrudes it will immediately feel out of place and you'll see it and remove it or adapt it until it fits into the 'Special World'.

It's important then to identify if, in the First Ten Pages, a 'Special World' is being created. From that will come much of the work that dominates so much of pre-production and which, done right, will create the glorious bubble you'll experience in production.

2. PROTAGONIST & ANTAGONIST

Amateur Writers are still introducing "important" characters on page 45 of their scripts. The audience isn't paying to see 30 minutes of unimportant characters before the film "gets going". They want to invest in the story quickly. They want to know who to root for and who the bad guy is. This might sound simplistic, but successful storytelling has a beautiful simplicity about it. It's sometimes difficult for writers to introduce both the Villain and the Good Guy within the first few pages, along with all the other principal characters — but it's a clear indication of the strength of the script.

An acceptable way around this problem is to be told about a Principal Character in such a way that his/her importance is clear to the audience and there is an expectation as to the character's nature. When the character finally appears, and the audience finds its expectation fulfilled — that's a fun moment. On the other hand, if the character is clearly not what has been anticipated because the descriptions were not quite accurate — that's even more delightful — and now the writer is Gear Shifting the audience!

Here's your First Ten checklist;

- *Genre will be fully in place.*
- *A Theme will be apparent or hinted at enough to build a possible Thematic Statement.*
- *There will have been an Ignition Event and the Story Engine will be in motion.*
- *The Pistons will be in moving and some Gear Shifts will have occurred.*
- *The Special World will have either been promised, or already introduced.*
- *The Principal Characters will have been heard from.*

There are entertainment professionals who will go no further than the First Ten if they cannot find these elements in place. There's a name for these people. We call them;

- *Successful Hollywood Players*

One of the problems of the First Ten Rule is in reading a script that truly excites and inspires your directorial energy, that seems to fulfill all the requirements of the First Ten and more — and then slumps around page 40 or 50 into a dragging, uninvolving series of less and less interesting events with a "resolution" that makes you wonder why you bothered to read the script in the first place.

Writers know, and fear, this dreadful manifestation as 'Act II flatness'.

It's disappointing, but unless there are big development dollars to bring on a rewrite team, and the possibility of talent attachments that will allow the money to flow until it's all fixed, the script that fails to deliver in the First Ten and then compounds the error by letting everything fizzle out in Act II usually requires only one comment from you.

'Pass'.

We've talked a great deal about the beginning of screenplays. Everything you've learned so far will help you to quickly winnow out the good from the bad and save you valuable time. It's also put you on a par with the majority of filmmaking professionals who need to read and understand scripts.

But what we've covered so far isn't quite enough to put you ahead of the pack and place you amongst the folks who know how to direct.

So, let's move onto the finer points.

CHAPTER SEVEN

Structure and Form

By now, in your reading of any script, you're able to identify Genre, create a Thematic Statement, observe the macro-movement of the Story Engine — whether the Pistons are in motion or not — and have an understanding of a vital micro-element, the Gear Shift. You are also able to check if a Special World is going to be presented and if the Principal Characters are on the first pages where they belong. We've sailed past page 10, so now we need to start paying attention to Structure and certain other interesting elements of Screenwriting Form.

1. FORM, NOT FORMULA

Good writing is about Form, not Formula. It doesn't have to hit specific waypoints using tired old constructions. That said, conventional wisdom suggests ideal structure for screenplays of between 90 and 120 pages is as follows;

- *Act I: Set Up. Pages 1-30. Plot Point between pages 25-27.*
- *Act II: Confrontation. Pages 30-90. Plot Point between pages 85-90*
- *Act III: Resolution. Pages 90-120*

This is acceptable 'Form' — but it tricks some writers into thinking that a screenplay is a series of marks they have to hit — and when that happens 'Form' becomes 'Formula'.

'Brightening His Room', that pivotal early scene in James Ivory's *The Remains Of The Day*, pushes us from Act I to Act II. It lasts around 3 minutes and begins 14 minutes into the film. According to the rules the Gurus have instilled in us, the important Gear Shift that Emma Thompson's 'Miss Kenton' makes initiates a 'Plot Point' and should have occurred around page 25 to 27. But in "Remains" it comes closer to page 17.

Not conventional.

- *Then why does it still work, and feel so natural?*

The answer is; Director Ivory and Screenwriter Ruth Prawer Jhabvala really paid attention to the First Ten. They got the audience so completely up-to-speed with Genre, Theme, Special World and Principals in those first pages that, as an audience, we were ready to go into Act II as early as page 17.

I mention this not just to illustrate the point that conventional wisdom should never become dogma, but because of the generalization that historical dramas set in English Country Houses are slow-moving to the point of tedium. Yet, *The Remains Of The Day* moves us quicker into Act II than the average Action Adventure movie — and way quicker than those formulaic "American" thrillers they used to go to Canada to shoot.

If you bear in mind that the three-act structure is a useful, but artificial, skeleton you'll remain open-minded enough to see when it's working and when it is not.

When it's *not* working the structure becomes a Frankenstein monster, with a skeleton fleshed out in all kinds of unlikely ways. In the worst of them you'll find gaping plot holes, jaw-dropping continuity problems and no room at all for interesting and original development of character or story. Also, when written to formulaic structure, bad scripts tend to reveal formulaic ideas and plots.

But, most interestingly, once you're aware that a screenplay has, or should have, definitive Acts, you'll also become aware when those Act Breaks occur — or not.

When you read a quality script, you'll feel that change happen — just as surely as you can hear a chord change when you're listening to music. In poorly written screenplays, you'll start to be conscious that the change hasn't come or doesn't work very well.

Go ahead and practice this. Read a script as you naturally would. If you feel the change, check out the Page number. Is it falling where it's expected to? If it shifts from Act I to Act II "early", then does it work? If "late", are there too many scenes that are holding up the movement, or are the scenes too long?

If you don't feel the Act change then go back to the area where the Gurus say the change should come (Pages 25/27 & 85/90). If you can't see the Act change in the place where we're told it's supposed to be, then search the neighborhood until you spot it. Again, if "early" or "late", check to see if it's a legitimate move. If you can't find the Act change at all, or if the demarcation line between Acts is so thin as to be barely there — you might be reading a screenplay that doesn't have good structure.

A screenplay with poor structure can be fixed, the story foundations made firmer — but it's almost a guarantee that if the structure isn't in good shape, the rest of the script will be wobbly. Kind of like a house. Bad foundation. Shaky building.

When a Writer has a good sense of Form, you will sense it in the reading. There will be nothing bloated about the screenplay. It will move smoothly and confidently. Duration of

Scenes, Sequences and Acts will feel right. The script becomes an easy read.

2. STRUCTURAL TERMINOLOGY

It's helpful to have a terminology when discussing screenplays with colleagues and collaborators. Good scripts unfold with beauty of Form and Structure because the writer understands the primary technical elements that go into the storytelling. Here they are;

BEAT: a moment in a scene where a character is in a process of change. (This is your Gear Shift).

SCENE: an event that unfolds in one location, or in perfect unity of time and place and which, ideally but not always, introduces a turning point in the story — a significant Piston movement. There may be three different Slug Lines, but you could treat it as a single scene if an actor starts in the basement, returns to the kitchen and ends up in the yard — provided there are no 'Time Cuts'.

As a Director you have to ask — *'What's happening in this scene? What's the point? How does it move the story forward?'* If a scene doesn't have a Piston movement, if nothing happens, then it's there for exposition, anticipation, to create a mood — or it's gone.

SEQUENCE: a series of Scenes. A writer will take the character(s) through a number of minor changes and shifts and bring us to a significant change by the end of the sequence. 'The Call To Adventure' which author Chris Vogler discusses in *The Writer's Journey: Mythic Structure for Writers* (Michael Weise Productions) is usually presented as a sequence.

Here's a typical 'Call To Adventure' sequence, which traditionally begins with the protagonist in denial or refusal mode;

Indiana Jones refuses to get involved. He's just back from his latest adventure and is not in the mood for another one. All he wants is some peace and quiet, so he comes up with reasons not to go on the latest escapade being thrust upon him. But the Call persists, and things are revealed that makes the invitation to adventure irresistible. It takes about four or five scenes, but the sequence inevitably ends with Indy back in the fedora en route to more trouble.

While there are sequences that are essentially movie tropes — the 'Call to Adventure', the 'Car Chase', the 'Shoot-Out' — there are also collections of scenes that cover a specific time frame or event, such as weddings or funerals and which must be regarded as sequences. Production Departments will certainly note that there's a 'wedding sequence', for example, because the unity of time and place will be important for every department from lighting and continuity, through to costuming, make-up and transport.

However, a Director may decide that the sequence begins at a time and place prior to the wedding itself and ends in a scene that takes place long after. For the Director in this case, the sequence isn't the event itself, but the emotional arc surrounding the event that affects the protagonists and/or antagonists.

You may find yourself with a script that intercuts two or more sequences, each with very different action and content. The juxtaposition of a gentle, quiet sequence with a sequence that is its antithesis is an extremely satisfying device. The one most enduring in my mind is the baptism/gangster assassination double-header in Francis Coppola's, *The Godfather* (Paramount, 1972).

As the Director you can't just move from scene to scene as you shoot and assume everything is going to fit together in perfect harmony. You must identify when a collection of scenes is a sequence, understand where the sequence starts and ends, find the beats where you will build towards the completion/climax of that sequence— and present it all with clarity. Yeah. Not easy.

ACT: a series of Sequences. A climax to what has gone before. In the Three Act structure favored by many writers, the end of Act II presents a major change, just when the problems seem to have been resolved. Act II to III is most often a large Piston Movement, with a big Gear Shift; *Indy was expecting to get out of this trouble fairly effortlessly. But now he's faced with an even more terrifying prospect, a situation that is almost hopeless.*

STORY: a series of Acts, which climaxes in a result that affects the lives of all the Principal Characters.

3. TIMING & TENSION

As a rule-of-thumb, one page of screenplay translates to one minute of screen-time. Thus, a 90-page screenplay will result in a film that runs an hour and a half.

In reality, the audience now takes in information much quicker — something I'll be discussing in greater detail in the further books in the series that deal with Performance and Editing. With more pace present in movies today, be aware that a page of screenplay often translates to about 45-50 seconds of screen-time.

As you read, try to be aware of how deep into the movie you will be in terms of time. If you've reached page 12 and it feels like it took forever, imagine how someone sitting in an audience will feel when a glance at a watch will reveal that the film has barely started.

The thing that keeps an audience from looking at their watches or sending a tweet to tell the world about the lameness of your movie, is Story Tension. To cement this concept in your mind, let us return to the early days of cinema.

4. THE GOLDBERG VARIATION

Back in the days when film first began to be projected commercially for mass audiences, filmmakers observed that a time period of 10 to 15 minutes seemed to hold an audience's attention very comfortably. Coincidentally — *or not* — the duration of a single 1,000' reel of film print running at 24 frames per second is 11 minutes, 6 seconds. At 18 f.p.s. (the frame rate most often used in the pioneer days) it's 14 minutes and 48 seconds

A 1000' reel, playing out in under 15 minutes, was capable of holding one "Story Tension". The hero is set up with a problem, faces some obstacles in overcoming the problem and finally resolves the problem. One Reel Wonder. Roll up. Pay your 5¢.

It's a Chicken and Egg story. What came first? The canny observation of Audience Attention Span or manufacturers — like the Goldberg Brothers — producing Reels in 1,000' lots?

Whatever the facts — and let's not allow facts to interfere with a good story — Goldberg Reels became an industry standard and Writers crafted stories to (a) fit the unit of allotted time and (b) maintain audience attention through the use of Story Tension. Producers, meanwhile, got together with marketing men and decided what audiences wanted to see. Which was a different thing entirely.

This being the film industry, it was discovered that audiences wanted more, and were prepared to pay for it. So, in true Hollywood style, things got doubled. Along came Two-Reelers, with *two* Story Tensions. In other words, a Sub Plot could be introduced with its very own Story Tension.

Once again you ask; *'So what?'*

Because, dear friends, as you read a submitted screenplay, you should be aware that a Goldberg Reel is passing every 11 pages or so and is definitely done by the end of every fifteenth page.

How was the Story Tension in the 11 or so pages you just read? Were there three, maybe four good Piston Movements that kept things moving along? Were there character Gear Shifts? At least two, maybe three or four? Did a new Story Tension begin to develop as the script started to pass into another Reel? Did your Act I contain one or two Reels? Or is this a lengthy, complex screenplay where Act I will require three Reels?

Can you use this Story Tension/Goldberg Reel concept to identify screenplays that have too much padding, or are too thin? You bet you can.

Can you use this concept to zoom in on a specific section of the screenplay and see if the mechanics are working properly and audience attention is going to be maintained? Absolutely.

Will using the Goldberg Variation help you to see *exactly* where the dreaded Act II flatness occurs? Yes, yes and yes!

Are you running out of highlight colors yet?

CHAPTER EIGHT

Sub Text

Sub-Text operates in a number of ways. Most noticeably, in performance art, it is an 'undertone' that speaks volumes. Often, it is information that not everyone in the scene "gets". Sometimes it's some knowledge shared between the *audience* and one or more of the characters that other characters do not know or understand. Occasionally, it's brought out with subtitles, narration or voice-overs whose content differs from what is being shown — or said by the actors. A blatant and over-the-top contemporary example would be the UK's *Peep Show* (Channel 4, 2003-2015) where the inner thoughts of the characters 'Mark' and 'Jez' are heard as voice-over in complete contradiction to what they are actually saying.

Sub-Text can be a convenient way for a writer to express something that cannot be expressed due to social conventions or political conditions. There's plenty of examples of writers getting very sexy and subverting, through Sub-Text, the strict moral guidelines of the old Hollywood Production Code. A sub-textural subversion that began in the 1930s and ran right up to the 60s and the introduction of the MPAA movie rating system.

On a scarier note, plenty of brave filmmakers, who haven't been lucky enough to live and work in the Land of the Free, have risked imprisonment and even death to bring truth to their audiences, shielded only by the flimsy cover of Sub-Text.

Sub-Text is also useful when the writer wants to allude to something that would seem too heavy-handed if laid out explicitly — a trick often seen in movies that want to convey a spiritual or religious message without beating the audience over the head with it.

Historical drama too, at its best, often has a Sub-Text that alludes to the present — but a present that it would be difficult or unwise to portray directly without the convenient camouflage of period costumes, coaches, swords and candlelight.

For example, a film like *The Duchess* (Paramount Vantage, 2008), Saul Dibbs' movie about an 18th Century British aristocrat, was seen by many as a veiled portrayal of England's Princess Diana. Francis Coppola's *The Godfather* could be said to have an allegorical Sub-Text alluding to how contemporary American corporate culture works, with its hierarchies and ruthless competiveness. Perhaps the most famous of these veiled references to contemporary figures through the lens of a historical reality is Orson Welles' *Citizen Kane* (RKO Radio Pictures, 1940) which comments on the ambition and lifestyle of newspaper magnate William Randolph Hearst and others of that ilk.

A close reading of a script, and an awareness of contemporary mores, conventions and conditions will quickly clue you to these kinds of literary Sub-Texts.

But let's move on to the real meat of Sub-Text. The Sub-Text that gives an actor oxygen.

A script that does not introduce, or suggest, performance-based Sub-Texts in considerable quantities is not worthy of your talents. Period. You're going to be working hard with your actors to bring a script to life, so why can't the writer work hard to take it at least some of the way there?

Actors develop performances from Sub-Text. Given that a Director is essentially the Head of the Acting Department, there's a Thespian Expectation that you'll present the Principal Players with scripts brimming with the stuff. If the Sub-Text is poorly contrived, the Actors may become uneasy or unruly. If there is no Sub-Text at all, panic might ensue. Free spirits who need gentle guidance might set off in entirely the wrong direction and need to be hauled back more roughly than usual. You don't want that.

Sub-Text is easy to identify, if you're looking.

- *Characters speak to each other, but what is really being said goes unspoken.*

It's in a pause, a look, or sometimes an inside knowledge that one of the characters, or the audience, has already understood.

Let me give you one of my crass examples.

Imagine a standard American Rom-Com and a storyline in which a shy but lovely young woman, 'Miranda', is about to go on an important job interview. In a previous scene, her 'Best Friend' takes her shopping (time for a montage!) and advises her on what to wear for this important interview. In an effort to boost the shy young woman's confidence, the friend persuades 'Miranda' to buy a skirt that is rather too short. At the interview, the incredibly good-looking employer/business owner 'Hugo' starts the meeting professionally and 'Miranda', awed by his gorgeousness, responds to his questions. However, she's conscious that her skirt is too short and she's regretting the choice. Her concentration is on that. The Writer will have given you Sub-Text Clues.

MIRANDA
(tugs the hem of her skirt)
Yes, I'm fully qualified in that area.

The Writer indicates with a parenthetical action (tugging the skirt) to Clue both Actor and Director (and by extension the Costume Department) to Miranda's embarrassed awareness. A Sub-Text that may continue to affect her concentration and confidence throughout the scene.

Now it's Hugo's turn for some Sub-Text. It might be written like this;

Miranda shifts in her seat. A long beat.

HUGO
Do you have any additional
marketing skills, Miss Jones?

Ah-ha! This is neutral. The writer has left the Sub-Text open for you and your actor. As written, Hugo is aware of how Miranda is dressed. It has been noted. But no Sub-Text exists. Is Hugo becoming inappropriately interested in Miranda and will the tone of the interview now become sexist to her further embarrassment and humiliation? Or is Hugo irritated at what he thinks is a blatant attempt by Miranda to get the job by using her sexuality. The writer could have Clued you in several different ways. Maybe like this...

Miranda shifts in her seat. A long beat.

HUGO
(smiles knowingly)
Do you have any additional
marketing skills, Miss Jones?

... or gone the other way, like this...

Miranda shifts in her seat. A long beat.

HUGO
(dismissive)
Do you have any additional
marketing skills, Miss Jones?

The important thing to realize is that the Sub-Text is not carried in the dialogue as it's written. It will be revealed in how the situation, the character, and the circumstances are interpreted. We're dealing with performance here, not with literature. The better writers will use a single word or phrase to give you the Sub-Text Clue. But this is only how the writer has imagined the scene will play. You might have a different idea — and so might your actors. Again, it's your choice how to proceed. If 'Hugo' is to be prim, proper and offended by 'Miranda' — then you, the Director, will no doubt find additional ways to convey the sub-textural characterization visually. You will cast, costume and design to suggest Hugo's cold professionalism and his disdain for women who show up for interviews with short skirts and long legs. In that instance, I'm seeing Colin Firth in pin-stripe business suit, rather than Matthew McConaughey in an open-neck shirt.

You don't need the Writer to spell out every detail (although some do). In the final analysis, you might not think that the writer's given Sub-Text is appropriate in the overall context of the script — so you'll change it.

In my example, two Clues were present to alert you to Sub-Text. 'Miranda' adjusting her skirt, and parenthetical directions given to 'Hugo' — dismissive, knowing, and neutral.

As our purpose here is to discuss 'Decoding', it's only important to spot Sub-Text clues in the reading and recognize them for what they are. We'll worry about how to interpret and direct them later.

Some Writers go overboard with Sub-Text clues —to the point where you feel they are directing the performances in their own heads and leaving nothing to be interpreted by Actors or Directors. — *Boo!*

Others deliberately hesitate to 'direct' — believing that Actors and Directors should be free to arrive at their own interpretations. — *Yay!*

A well-written script will have its Sub-Text elements very carefully balanced and placed and will leave no doubt where the writer is taking the characters and what she wants them to understand.

CHAPTER NINE

Texture

Professional screenplays suggest 'Texture' to the Director. If texture doesn't hold any interest for you, you may as well direct broadcast television sit-com or daytime soap — as these forms hold little or no 'Texture'.

That last sentence sounded aggressive and dismissive — but it was deliberately stated in that way to grab your attention. There is not a single internationally known Director who is not also a master of 'Texture'. The Directors who care little for this important element are legion — and have had far less impact on audiences.

When you take the story off the page and put it in front of the camera, 'Texture' is a primary tool in wrapping the world of the story around your audience and allow them to viscerally 'feel' your movie. The proper use of 'Texture' *always* separates good directors from the indifferent.

You'll find 'Texture' in script descriptions — the brief sentences that capture a detail of mood or atmosphere. Details that suggest something observed in life which, combined with the story, makes the Special World stronger and more vibrant. 'Textural' details help and — in a sense — give you permission to build powerful images into your movie. Directors can add

'Texture' into projects that have none, but if a Writer hasn't been skilled enough to give them to you, chances are the script is inadequate in other departments too.

If the Writer *hasn't* given you some 'Texture', you're on your own. Some directors prefer scripts that do not include textural elements — because they're very conscious of being allowed to interpret a script towards something that satisfies their own instincts and creativity. My argument runs counter to this. I want 'Texture'. Lots of it. A script without texture is like porridge without salt. For the non-Scottish amongst you, that means — it has no flavor.

Now, I can always change, adjust or remove that flavor — I'm the Director after all, which is why in this business you will see the credit *'A Film by Markus Innocenti'* and the Writer barely gets mentioned. (But in a collaborative medium good work depends on collaboration. And the first collaboration you will encounter is with the Writer, so try not to get too up on yourself).

As you come across descriptions in the screenplay you're reading, examine them for the "visual" effect they have on you and whether the description truly helps you see the Special World of the story better.

Many times, you're going to run straight into cliché. Cemetery scenes in the rain. Lovers strolling down lanes with autumnal leaves falling. Killers escaping up metal steps in abandoned warehouses.

They were all good the first time.

It takes a better than average screenwriter to give a director Clues to 'Texture' that will actually result in some freshness. But, one of the downsides of the 'business' end of movie-making is that you'll find a lot of scripts out there where the writer has shied away from short descriptions that would add texture — usually because he or she is aware that the majority of people who read scripts have no respect for a well-turned phrase, or an original description that will spark a director's synapses.

The written word is disrespected, and Writers —sensitive souls that they are — are hesitant to put something as luxurious as 'Texture' on paper and risk an impatient reaction from an Executive or an under-paid Studio Reader. Like so many other things in contemporary filmmaking, 'Texture' is a craft detail that is pushed along the pipeline for someone else to sort out. The Production Designer and the Director. The Visual Effects Supervisor, the Cinematographer and sometimes The Stunt Coordinator.

It's reached the point where we've come to believe that 'Texture' is no longer the province of Writers. You start to get used to it, then you pick up a script by a novice Writer with no battle scars. She'll give you 'Texture' by the yard because nobody's told her not to — yet. Unfortunately, more often than not, novice Writers fall into visual clichés because, like so many of us, their internal wide screen keeps projecting images they've seen in films, instead of visual experiences they've had in life.

I have to go off on a tangent for a moment. Here's the problem. When creative people — like Writers — are placed in a position where they are being advised *not* to do something, then the thing they are *not doing* has to be done by someone else. That someone else is usually the designated expert — who most often has a tried-and-true formula that worked on the last fifty pictures so it should be good enough for you.

Right?

Wrong.

Let me give you an example — bearing in mind that my rants are generally generic, and that exceptions abound. Take fight sequences. Most good Writers are capable of writing a scenario that would be fresh, original and — most importantly — bring to the sequence the various layers of Genre, Theme, Sub Text, Structure, Form and all the other good things we're looking for.

But.

They are told not to clutter up the screenplay with dense paragraphs of description. Instead they must merely write;

```
        Joe and Jack fight. Joe is beaten to a
pulp.
```

This sentence allows the Suits to agree that by hiring a known Fight Coordinator they'll have a superb punch-up to thrill the masses. Basking in the simplicity of it, and without having to have gone through the tedium of reading more than a single line… it's time for lunch.

Yes, yes. I know. I'll never work in Hollywood again.

You see, once the Writer has been forced to abdicate a creative role then the Director has been robbed of an opportunity to read and understand a Writer's viewpoint (his mental pictures put on paper) as to how this fight would, or should, develop and conclude.

The problem now is the *possibility* that the Fight Coordinator will work out the Joe/Jack fight perhaps without fully understanding the respective strengths, weaknesses and motivations of the characters. Directors and Cinematographers will have input, of course — but the sequence now *belongs* to the Fight Coordinator.

While many Stunt/Fight Coordinators and VFX folks are as much concerned with 'creative' aspects as they are with 'technical', it is the Director's responsibility to make sure things stay on course — and this is sometimes discouraged. A demarcation line gets drawn, and the sequence is taken out of the Director's hands because (s)he is "not an expert". So, now *two* key creatives — Writer and Director — are no longer involved.

This, in my opinion, is why so many fight scenes (and many love scenes) are incredibly tedious. There's been a ton of 'technical thinking', but some of the creative team have been left out of the process.

In fairness, I should mention that there are some screenwriters, of A-list quality generally, who have overcome this problem. In one of his screenplays, Shane "*Lethal Weapon*" Black gives the kind of bald, single sentence description I've described but then throws the decision for how a scene will be executed to the people who have to do the creative work — namely, the director and the actors — and gives them all the information they need by adding; '*this is not a love scene; this is a sex scene*'. To cement the idea that it's not his place to 'interpret', he goes on to suggest that the actors will likely have 'highly athletic ideas' that would surpass anything a writer could imagine. Interestingly, Mr. Black devotes a full 4/8ths of a page explaining in amusing ways why he is *not* going to write this love/sex scene — which neatly indicates how much screen-time he feels should be devoted to it.

Thank you for allowing this digression. Normal service will now resume.

1. UNMISTAKABLE TEXTURE

'Texture' on the page has a remarkable effect when it's well done. By well done, I mean it's usually very pithy, very precise. It evokes a clear image in the mind's eye. It makes a script come to life. I offer an example from *The Hunt For Red October* (Paramount Pictures, 1990) written by Larry Ferguson and Donald Stewart.

Here, using unorthodox Sluglines, is how the screenplay opens;

A BARREN LANDSCAPE
beneath a slate-grey sky. Frigid rock and stunted trees fall to an ice-choked coast. Congealed sea on a desolate beach.

MARKO ALEXANDROVICH RAMIUS
bare-headed in cold wind, studies the inclement coast. Bottomless eyes move slowly across the landscape, missing nothing.

Note the power of that first paragraph. 23 words to describe a location so completely you will instantly "feel" the cold and the isolation. Menace too perhaps. 23 words that will send the location department scurrying. That will already have the cinematographer thinking about lenses, contrast and dynamic range. 23 words that will tell everyone that reads it this is a "big" picture, perhaps "epic". 23 words that suggest 'genre' in as much as a "barren landscape" and harsh environment already points to 'Action' and 'Adventure'. 23 words that immediately take you into a 'Special World'. Amongst those 23 words are phrases like "Congealed sea on a desolate beach" and compound words like "ice-choked". Pithy. Precise. Literary — but without pretention. And —vitally — filled with 'Texture'. All this and only 23 words into the script.

Now, the second paragraph. 20 words. Introducing, judging by the character naming in the unconventional slug line, a Principal character. What do we learn about this character in 20 words? Uncaring or impervious to the cold — suggesting he is a man of action or has things on his mind that make comfort unimportant. He "studies" the coast. Suggesting experience perhaps — or anxiety? Why does someone "study" a "barren landscape"? We are being invited to read on and find out. His eyes are "bottomless" and "missing nothing". Are you intrigued yet? Do you want to know more about this man?

43 words. Not all of them spoke to 'Texture' — but enough were dropped into this opening to tell the director that the writers were right there with him in establishing a Special World that would wrap around the audience.

In the film that director John McTiernan made from this screenplay, the "ice-choked" coast is fully present. Ramius (played by Sean Connery) is first seen in an ECU of his eyes "missing nothing". The only difference is that Mr. Connery is not "bare-headed in cold wind". The director knew that costuming the actor in a Russian fur cap with naval insignia would be a stronger visual 'Texture', conveying both the cold, the authority and the genre.

2. TRANSLATING FROM PAGE TO SCREEN

Want to know what 'Texture' should look like when it's taken off the page? Watch the films Ridley Scott made between 1977 and 1982. All of David Fincher's films are wall-to-wall 'Texture'. The Coen Brothers won't shoot a frame without an almost obsessive regard for 'Texture'.

Sometimes, particularly in 'Low-Budget' productions, the more obvious 'Textures' — graffiti-daubed buildings, rusting steel, peeling paint and the like — become a lazy visual shorthand which requires care when lifted off the page and put in the frame, because they've been over-used or are simply there to look 'cool'.

The elements themselves are *always* 'Textures'. Wind, Water, Fire, Earth, Metal. Being so basic, so primal, these 'Elemental Textures' lift images beyond the ordinary and help performance. Rain is the classic example. A detective trying to track a suspect through driving rain is a great deal more interesting than the same action on a clear, sunny day.

Any mention of 'rain' and I automatically think of Akira Kurosawa — which shows how deeply a 'Texture' element can sink into the psyche and define a filmmaker. Rain is the predominant and stunning 'Texture' in Kurosawa's *Seven Samurai* (Columbia Pictures, 1956), while heat, harsh sunlight and dust are the primary 'Textures' for John Sturges' American remake, *The Magnificent Seven* (United Artists, 1960).

To summarize; 'Texture' should be present in a script — and in the film you make — to create mood and atmosphere. But its purpose is to amplify a Story Tension or make the 'Special World' more defined and unique.

There *has* to be an underlying meaning or purpose.

The caveat is; when you come across 'Texture' in a script examine it carefully. If you find that the writer has used 'Texture' as a quick visual shorthand — chances are it's also clichéd and banal.

Some 'Textures' become fashionable and over-used — and end up looking contrived when the footage lands in the edit room. It'll pay dividends to read with the awareness that you might be getting steered in the wrong direction.

CHAPTER TEN

Image and Aural Systems

Advanced screenwriters will sometimes build internal subliminal systems into their scripts that, if implemented correctly, make the resulting film more powerful.

Sometimes, the best way of understanding what something is, is to first understand what it is not. Image and Aural Systems are not 'symbols' or 'symbolic'. If a writer ends a scene like this;

Jack sits at the table, staring at a bowl of decaying fruit. He feels dead inside.

Then it is fairly certain that the writer is using the bowl of decaying fruit to symbolize 'death' and we're supposed to think; *'Ah-hah! Jack is feeling dead inside —check out the fruit!'* That's not a System. Especially if it's the only time we see, or reference, decaying fruit in the screenplay or final film.

But if an elderly mafia boss is shot down in the street having just purchased a bag of oranges, and if —much later in the film — he's fooling around with an orange just before he dies... then, chances are, that's a System and you should probably go back and look at the film again and find the System elements you didn't consciously 'see' the first time.

Careful though. Sometimes it's neither a System nor a Symbol, but a 'Leitmotif'. A 'leitmotif' is a device (usually, but not always, musical) associated with a character and location and, in rare cases, with a situation or idea.

The familiar use of a 'leitmotif' is in Opera, Musical Comedy and Film Soundtracks. Characters or situations have particular musical phrases associated with them at every appearance. What matters about a 'leitmotif' from our perspective isn't who or what it is associated with, but the fact that it *recurs*. Over and over. Until it is obvious to the audience — and that very obviousness becomes enjoyable in itself.

In the hands of Composers and/or Sound Designers 'Leitmotifs' can happily exist in feature films, (unlike their nefarious cousins, the Symbols). Their purpose is to reinforce character, location, situation and the 'idea' of the scene. The Movie Franchises, for example, use 'leitmotifs' constantly.

The broad rule to remember is this. If something is a Big, Deliberate and Obvious Placement in the film, it's either a 'Symbol' or a 'Leitmotif'. If it makes you cringe, then it's likely a 'Symbol'. If it recurs in such a way to both contribute to your enjoyment and play on your basic emotional senses — then it's probably a 'Leitmotif'.

- *So, what is an Image System exactly?*

This is a mouthful, but here goes. An Image System is a systemic visual device, most often created by a film director but sometimes by a skilled screenwriter. An Image System works subliminally. It supports and underpins the Special World, the situation, and the concerns of the characters and the dominant theme(s) of the film.

An Image System should never be immediately obvious to the audience, even though it's right there in front of them. It should be so much a part of the action that it is over-looked —

but, and this is the important part, it makes a strong contribution to the feelings the audience experiences.

The more subliminal the writer and/or director keeps the System, the harder it may be to identify — but it will undoubtedly be 'stronger' and more interesting.

That's why any Image or Aural Systems described in a screenplay should never be presented as Big Symbols. If you find "symbolism" in the script you're reading (sadly, it's all too obvious) you have to raise your internal red warning flag. Symbols are not going to help you in the long run.

Plainly put, it is extremely hard to introduce a Symbol into a film without making it look contrived and clichéd.

Far better to build an Image System. But how?

1. BUILDING THE IMAGE SYSTEM

To get us in the mood, here's a couple of examples of Image Systems created by master filmmakers.

John Boorman's crime thriller, *Point Blank* (MGM, 1967) is my go-to example. Love this movie. It's the story of 'Walker' (played by Lee Marvin) who determinedly goes after the men who betrayed him, seeking to recover stolen money he considers to be rightfully his.

Boorman introduces a System into the film that subliminally gives the audience an understanding, a feeling, of how difficult and frustrating Walker's search is. It's a System all about "Seeing", or rather — "Not Seeing".

Here's just a few of the ways he does it;

(i) Bright headlights dazzle Walker, confusing him and not allowing him to see what's going on. (ii) A dirty screen door obscures a clear view of an important action. (iii) A misty morning prevents Walker from identifying a killer. (iv) Distance makes another identification impossible.

It's a bold and beautifully rendered System, deliberately introduced, which reinforces the film's Theme and plays into the Principal character's Sub-Texts of frustration, anger and single-mindedness.

Roman Polanski's *Chinatown* (Paramount Pictures, 1974) has an interesting System. This time it's "Reflections". Sunlight reflected off metal at the bottom of a pond gives 'Jake Gittes' (played by Jack Nicholson) a major piece of information. A man Jake is keeping under observation is seen reflected in the lenses of Jake's binoculars. Shots are set up using reflections in chrome, or mirrors. It's a System amplifying in a subtle way the whole concept and Theme of the film — that everything we see is not what it appears to be. That all is somehow backwards or distorted and not true.

Here's a 6-point approach that may help:

1. Throw out the unnecessary 'Symbols' if they are present in the script. Generally, this is the director's job, although a rewrite screenwriter can take care of it too.

2. If you spot an Image System already present in the screenplay then consider carefully how appropriate it is. Is it subtle? Does it reinforce theme and character concerns? Can it be shot in a way that allows it to be almost unnoticed?

Now that we're free of 'Symbols', and have determined that the writer hasn't built an 'Image System'...

3. Assemble the building bricks for your System by focusing on the theme of the screenplay, and by examining what the principal characters have to overcome to get to their result. Where are the challenges? The frustrations, the joys? How are the pivotal scenes staged? What kind of locations will there be

for the important dialogue exchanges, or the intense action scenes? What else is going on in those scenes?

4. An Image System is a specialized form of 'Texture', layered unobtrusively into screenplay or film. It's a layer designed to play upon the psychological, internal senses of the reader or audience. What do you want the audience to feel at certain moments? Unease? Amusement? Whatever it is, can an Image System enhance those feelings?

5. If it's conceived and presented in a methodical yet delicate manner, a good System always remains 'felt' more often than it is consciously 'seen'. As your Image System concept becomes more and more apparent to you, make sure it can fit into the world of the film in such a way that it becomes almost unnoticeable because of its seeming 'ordinariness'.

6. Chose a word or short phrase to help you — rather like you earlier chose the sentence that became your Thematic Statement.

To give an example, one of the pictures I'm currently attached to direct is an ensemble piece. A multi-character relationship story. It's set in a single location — a struggling business. No Image System is present in the script, but if I build a System using the phrase "Nothing Works", then I'm going to have some fun introducing an extremely varied element that can be as subtle as I want it to be, and subliminally reinforce the story's themes, inter-character relationships and viewpoint.

In Chapter 13 I'll give you some further real-world examples, because I know 'Image System' is a difficult concept to get comfortable with. But I hope you're already starting to see how it can be a very powerful tool to add to your filmmaking skillset.

2. SOUND FOR VISION

An Aural System isn't always the province of the composer or music supervisor — although music can be considered an Aural System. Novice screenwriters sometimes imagine their role is to select music — largely because they have an idea of what would be appropriate for a character or situation. No harm, no foul — but incredibly unlikely that anyone would ever pay attention to what a writer has to say about music choices in a film — unless, of course, the writer is also the director and/or producer, or the screenplay is about a specific music or musician.

I'll talk more about the function of Sound in a further book in this series — but there's a degree of difference between creating an Aural System and a post-production sound-designed Aural Signature.

An Aural Signature might be something the audience hears very clearly and distinctly in association with a particular character or location — a 'Leitmotif'. An Aural System, on the other hand, is something that is subliminally 'felt' rather than consciously 'heard'. It is most often used for specific emotional purposes — just as Boorman's Image System in "Point Blank" reinforced his character's emotional condition.

To give you some examples; a cold ambience might be used to reinforce a character's isolation. The sound of drips, water running, toilets flushing, showers being taken, rain hitting windows — all could underscore points in the story and create specific emotional reactions. The various sounds of animals might help important plot shifts. An array of deep, almost inaudible, rumbles or electrical hums could create senses of alienation or tension. A variety of metallic sounds might suggest something about the character or the situation and play on the audience's emotional responses. The amount of 'metal' in Andrei Tarkovsky's *Stalker* (Mosfilm, 1979) is excruciating, painful and deadening in its variety and relentless presence. And completely wonderful.

Were the Image and Aural Systems I've mentioned present in the original scripts? In some cases, yes. They were gifts from the Writer should the Director choose to use them. If the scripts didn't have Systems described, then the Director did what s/he was inclined to do — given the interpretation of the screenplay and the Thematic Statement s/he was intent on proving — and added a System layer to give the final film more depth and impact.

No Systems? No Problem. It's not a deal breaker if you can't find one in the pages you're reading. If all that's missing in the script is the hint of an Image or Aural System for you to develop — and everything else is in place — then you've still got a decent screenplay to work with.

There's something I should include here before we leave this chapter and mentioning Tarkovsky reminds me of it. I've gone to some length to make you aware that heavy-handed use of Symbols is not attractive. I believe that most often a Symbol takes the audience "out of the picture" for a moment. I binge-watched a superb television episodic recently. After 73 hours of some of the greatest writing, acting and direction I've ever seen on television, the filmmakers decided to use some "powerful" Symbols in the concluding sequence of the series. Talk about putting a foot through a Rembrandt. 'Dearie me', as my Scots mother would say, with a sigh.

But there is an element in some of the greatest films in international cinema that *appears* to be a 'Symbol' due to the emphasis placed on it, usually through the duration of the shot — the way the shot lingers on something that appears to be of no real importance. Many of the master directors use this element — names like Tarkovsky, Antonioni and Ozu — although you'd be hard-pressed to think of an American director who would do so. Lynch perhaps, and sparingly.

The element I'm talking about is not an Image System, it's not a Leitmotif and it's not a Symbol. It often looks like an

Establishing shot. But it's not. It could be a shot of a bird on a wire. Or a vase standing in a window alcove. A cat sitting on a wall. A woman leaning out of her window. A street lamp. The element has been described by film critics as a 'Pillow Shot' — originally in their discussions of Yasujiro Ozu's films.

The purpose of the 'Pillow Shot' is to allow the audience's emotional response to what they have just seen to deepen exponentially. It's a shot that allows the audience to reflect, to be still for a moment in the afterglow of a previous scene's emotional impact. It allows one's own mind, however unconsciously, to catch up and truly feel the enormity of what has gone before. In many cases, it produces a meditative state in an audience that allows them a new, and perhaps novel, understanding of the world or a circumstance that hadn't been fully thought of before.

In other words, a 'Pillow Shot' plays with audience's most internal thought processes and feelings —provided the audience is willing to be receptive. To me, it's an astonishing and wonderful thing that film is capable of doing something so profound.

But.

It has to be accepted that, for most audiences, film is a predominantly passive journey into the story being told, it's not a gateway to deeper understandings or active self-revelation. That's why you'll find many people involved in film — and not just in the United States — who are impatient and dismissive of forms of filmmaking that seek to take their audiences into new emotional territory. The 'Pillow Shot' is a bridge too far for most producers looking to get returns on the investment — and the situation hasn't been helped by filmmakers who have attempted to use a very delicate and sophisticated filmic element without fully understanding what they are doing.

The 'Image System' is a much more user-friendly device and my suggestion would be to master it before moving on to attempt a 'Pillow Shot'.

Guess what. You've now gone through all the elements a Director needs to evaluate the worthiness of a script.

- *Really? We're done? Checklist, please!*

Ahm, no. Hate to tell you. There's a little more work to do.

CHAPTER ELEVEN

More Detective Work

Your first reading will allow you to determine if the script you've been handed is direct-able, needs a major re-write, or should go in the trash.

It's that simple.

If you've followed all the information up to this point, you will now be able to read a script like a Director. You'll be confident that you can make a good decision on whether a project is worth being attached to. You'll know if a script requires re-writing — and be able to make strong suggestions as to where the weakness lies.

Most importantly, you'll have an awareness of the following key elements and how they work;

- Genre
- Thematic Statement
- The Story Engine
- Structure and Form
- Sub-Texts
- Texture
- Image and Aural Systems
- The First Ten

The ability to understand and implement this checklist puts you amongst the professionals.

Remember I started out by insisting that only you — the Director — would ever read a script for what it really is?

We're now going to examine those elements that everyone *else* is excited about. They think what they've noticed is the entire thing. Bless 'em. But really, what everybody besides the director notices in a script is not much more than a shopping list of 'must-haves' and 'gotchas' that in themselves don't signify whether a screenplay is suitable for professional production or not.

As we've already discovered, great scripts are full of amazing little Clues that make interpreting them a joy. Less well-wrought efforts have badly conceived Clues, formulaic Clues or no Clue at all.

We've already seen Clues that will take us a long way to putting the screenplay up on a screen. We had Clues that helped us understand what kind of film we're making (Genre). We've been given a Clue to find a way through the story and arrive at a 'result' (Thematic Statement). We're Clued into whether the story will work or not (Story Engine, Structure and Form). We've been given Clues to help us find the "real" concerns of the story and the characters. Using them we'll be able to assist our Actors (Sub-Text). We've been given Clues that allow us to construct a 'World' for our story and for our characters to live in (Texture, Image and Aural Systems).

But, wait. There's more.

CHAPTER TWELVE

Here Comes Captain Obvious

I apologize, but in the interests of full disclosure, and a determination to avoid as many emails as possible from my readership demanding to know why I haven't mentioned such-and-such, there now follows a series of points raised by our pedantic friend, Captain Obvious.

The Captain has identified the following issues that arise in the reading of a screenplay and demands that these be addressed;

- Casting & Character
- Locations
- Cost, Time & Schedule
- Props, Sets & Picture Vehicles
- Dialogue
- Pace & Rhythm
- Character Naming

When you direct, you become an answering machine. Every single person working on the film needs to know what's on your mind to the extent that it guides their input. On larger productions, the content of your mind is filtered downwards from your Department Heads. Given that these are professional and capable people, you better be ready to answer their questions. You need to be able to respond.

The Clues lurking in the script will give you that Response Ability. However, these particular Clues are apparent to everyone, so trouble can arise.

Why?

Because everybody has their own 'vision' and is excited by that 'vision'. It sometimes takes a while for the less experienced to understand that the only 'vision' that matters is yours.

1. CASTING & CHARACTER

To give a quick example of how things can go wrong, let's imagine that the Writer has tossed in a Clue to 'Character' — and, by extension 'Casting'. In the screenplay, let's suppose a role is introduced like this;

MARGO (38), the elegant and svelte hostess, moves amongst the new arrivals bestowing air-kisses and cries of delight.

What you 'see' from this Clue may be considerably different from your collaborators. It's at this point that you will find out how powerful you are, and how much your input is listened to and respected. Many times, decisions will be made that are far removed from your original 'vision' and are often taken out of the Director's control entirely. And there are times when a decision can't be reached until the last moment for all kinds of reasons from budget to availability.

Even the best Directors often don't know what they want until they see it, but when your collaborators present something to you — a location, a casting, a prop — you have to measure what they are showing you against your original 'vision' and instincts.

Then, either accept it or dismiss it.

If you 'accept' something because you are compromising for the sake of budget, availability, time, cost, a desire to be easy to work with — or whatever reason —you better be sure that your compromise will not diminish the script, or your 'vision' for the film.

Compromise too much, or too readily, and your collaborators will pick up the scent of your weakness very quickly.

What this is leading up to is really a warning. Be aware that this secondary list of Clues is especially important to your collaborators because it's through these Clues that they do *their* work. You have to lead the team. It's vital you pay serious attention to the Clues that make an impression on others.

When you see one of these 'Captain Obvious' Clues — Margo, the elegant and svelte socialite — you need to bring it fully into your 'vision' so you can guide everyone onto a perfect result, or you need to adjust the descriptive Clue as soon as possible to prevent it becoming too deeply, and wrongly, embedded in your team's 'vision'.

This section of *The Filmmaker's Art* is about "Decoding The Script", so I'm not going to devote space to 'Casting' beyond what I've already stated above. 'Casting' is a particularly thorny issue which I'll go into later. All that matters for now is that, while you're reading, you should pay close attention to those 'Casting & Character' Clues and develop a viewpoint that you can defend.

If you don't, one day the Production Pistons will move without you and give you the kind of Gear Shift that feels like you got grit poured in your transmission.

2. LOCATIONS

A little further on the in the screenplay, the writer has described a location;

A solitary acacia tree stands on the hilltop, overlooking a bend in the river.

This is a slightly different issue from the 'Casting & Character' problem. Nobody ever raised money on a picture by "attaching" a location. Well, probably not. 'Casting' might already be a 'fait accompli' by the time you get hired, but you can be fairly sure that locations are going to be presented to you for a decision. After all, the producer is expecting you to translate or interpret the images present in the script and do so within her budget.

All of which means that this is a Clue which can unseat you very badly. It doesn't matter if the Clue is for an acacia tree on a hilltop by a river bend, or a graffiti-emblazoned abandoned warehouse in a harbor — you have to get it right or risk losing the mood of the film and the respect of the audience. There are a million different ways to find and shoot the acacia tree, but they're dependent on budget and they're dependent on 'will' — the determination of you and your producer to bring that single line in the script to the screen in such a way that it 'works'.

Now, if you're David Lean you ship your cast and crew to a wild and distant location and wait three weeks for the sun to hit the acacia tree in just the right way and for the river to be flowing below at just the right speed. If you're Stanley Kubrick, you import a tree from sub-Saharan Africa, order up 500 tons of dirt, gravel and sand to build the hilltop on a barge in the center of London and then divert the River Thames to bend past your camera just the way you "saw" it.

If you're a more contemporary filmmaker on a modest budget, you'll jump in your SUV with a camera and go find a river bend. Shoot it, then go find an acacia tree. Set the camera at the correct angle and throw green screen in the background.

Voilà.

The point is — as the Director — you need to read the descriptive line and have the confidence of knowing how to shoot it. Because if you aren't confident that you can bring the writer's mental image to the screen, then you just might have a problem.

Unless you and your producers are prepared not to care.

In which case, it doesn't really matter if it's an acacia tree on a hilltop above a river bend at all, does it? And does it have to be a hilltop? Do we really need a river in the shot?

3. COST, TIME & SCHEDULE

Try to read your script with an awareness that everything costs time and money. If your script features huge chase sequences, multiple locations, major visual effects sequences, hundreds of extras — better have a budget that can cope with that. Don't waste your time reading a script that is beyond the budgets that you are going to get. Or rather, *do* read it to get a sense of what a larger, financially ambitious screenplay is doing — and see if it's following all the rules. There are legions of wannabee directors, writers and producers out there who cannot grasp the fact that the project they're getting so excited about is going to cost $60m to make. Sure, get excited if there is a reasonable chance of raising the funding and you can remain attached to the project. But if it's an unlikely proposition, wait to make the project when you're at a level in the industry where that kind of money will seek you out.

Don't waste your time now on something financially un-realistic. Find a project that you can do *now* with the resources that are going to be made available to you.

As you gain more on-set experience, or if you already have a good idea of production costs and budgeting then — as you read — you'll start to see how much the project might cost.

Perhaps the project is already funded, and you already know how much money you have to play with. In which case, examine that screenplay and try to see where the money is go-ing to go. If something concerns you — ask questions. Don't be caught agreeing to do something and find out later that it's just not viable for the money available.

On larger productions, you'll be asked to 'sign off' on the budget. That's a written, legal agreement that you are aware of the budget, you've studied the account details and are confirming that you can take the project from page to screen while staying within the agreed funding limits.

If a project is not fully funded, then you're going to have to hope that the producers have a realistic understanding of how much it will cost to turn this particular script into light and shadows. In either case, limitations imposed by the available funding will become apparent. It's how you overcome these obstacles that will define you as a filmmaker.

This brings us neatly to issues of Time & Schedule. *Selecting For Success*, the next title in *The Filmmaker's Art* series deals with this topic in very great detail. For now, as you're reading, you can 'decode' by making a good estimate of how fast you're going to have to work.

If you have a 100-page script and you think you could shoot 5 pages a day, then simple math informs us that you will need 20 days of Principal Photography. If you've already been told you have a mere 12 days to shoot, you might want to pause and consider where and how you're going to speed up to make a daily schedule of over 8 pages.

4. PROPS, SETS & PICTURE VEHICLES

Imagine you have one of our 'Captain Obvious' Clues that places a scene in a tunnel during the Viet Nam war. In the scene, the tunnel collapses onto two G.I.s.

Everything boils down to bucks. In your 'vision' of this scene, how do you want to shoot it? What do you request from your Producer and Production Departments?

You're going to get many suggestions. Creatively, the most important will be coming from your Cinematographer, your Production Designer/Art Director and, in this case, your Stunt Coordinator. But the bottom line is always going to be the business of making it happen within the financial limitations of the project. Which is why the Line Producer is hovering so nervously.

There are a million ways to shoot this 'Tunnel Rat' scene. Some directors will immediately think of doing it digitally on a green screen stage. With my production design experience, my own first thoughts are 'build a set', so I can track cameras, light naturalistically and control everything. Others might want to explore actual locations — or use a combination of physical and digital. You could probably build a set for this scene in a backyard in Glendale, California for under $300. Actually, there's no doubt about it — it's been done. You could just as easily spend $150,000.

Let's read deeper into this scene and think about the details. We have two G.I.s in a Viet Cong tunnel. How are they equipped? How are they dressed? Does their period costuming have markings or insignia? What weapons are they carrying? Will the production, and its key crew, have the time, money and resolve to get all these details correct and authentic?

Something else can blindside you and it's similar to having a Casting choice forced upon you. Occasionally, you get someone high up on the food chain reading the script and getting all excited about a prop, a picture vehicle, some costuming — even a location. They just happen to have access to some amazing thing that will add production value. *In their opinion*. Generally, that 'thing' — a Ferrari, for example — looks pretty darn exciting but detracts from the picture because it is so out of place. Unless a Ferrari is specified in the script, and makes sense, you're going to have to veto it and make someone important feel disappointed and — perhaps — slighted.

Do you begin to see how the simplest of 'Captain Obvious Clues', in a script that maybe is not fully realized or thought-out, can result in a battle of wills between you and any number of people who have come onto the project?

5. DIALOGUE

Dialogue has been placed in the 'Captain Obvious' list for two reasons. First, most everybody knows bad dialogue when they read it. It's, well — obvious. Second, if the story is there — real, immediate and present — then poor dialogue can be fixed, so no need to put it in our Primary list because it isn't necessarily a reason for you to 'pass' on a script. Heck, there are some directors who can make pretty good movies without the benefit of scripted dialogue — relying entirely on actors working on a suggested scene or storyline and building the dialogue through improvisation and rehearsal. Here's some points to consider;

(a) SILENCE IS GOLDEN

Watch for characters who talk too much. We're dealing with motion pictures — not the theatre. Good writers are sparing in their use of dialogue. Less is always more. Hitchcock

knew this very, very well. Remember, he began his career in silent films (*The Pleasure Garden*, 1925) and directed the UK's
first "talkie"(*Blackmail*, 1929). Because Hitchcock first told his
stories without dialogue, his visual sense was, and remained,
acute. He deplored early "talkies" which, to him, were nothing
more than filmed stage-plays.

So, the question to ask yourself is; could this script
work without dialogue? A screenplay whose story could largely
play out without dialogue is a powerful screenplay indeed.
Those which are heavy on dialogue — particularly big thick,
page-long chunks of dialogue — need to be approached with
caution and reservation. Unless you're Ingmar Bergman.

(b) REMOVE NORMAL

You'll hear the term 'on-the-nose'. Beginning Screenwriters get very anxious about making their stories 'under-
standable', so they use dialogue to put the message across.
This is a usage of 'on-the-nose' dialogue that performs a similar function as Exposition — which is a character giving us
background on the plot that we have no previous knowledge of
or explaining something that we have seen but not yet fully understood. But the main reason beginning Screenwriters tend to
have 'on-the-nose' dialogue is because they want their characters to speak 'normally' so as to make them 'real', and because
they are finding it difficult to ease the characters into a situation
where the plot moves on.

Clearly, dialogue shouldn't make the movie stand still,
but not every exchange of dialogue has to move the story forward. That can get exhausting. The fault lies in a writer trying to
make his characters speak like *real human beings* — without
realizing that, in movies, dialogue can never be 'normal'. If we
follow Hitchcock's admonition that movies are *real life with the
boring bits cut out*, then movie dialogue shouldn't be boring.

Ever.

In a later book in *The Filmmaker's Art* series, I'll be discussing how filmmakers need to compress everyday actions — through blocking, shooting techniques and editing — to remove the boring physical things that would be tedious to show. It is equally tedious to go through the same old 'Hi, how are you'/'Great - how're you doin'?/Oh, I'm good" dialogue exchanges in screenplays. The removal of the everyday is vital.

Truly skillful writers can still give us long screeds of dialogue — I'm thinking of Quentin Tarantino and Woody Allen — but there will be nothing 'normal' about what is being said. The characters will gradually be more fully revealed, and some kind of Story Tension will be developing. Pistons Moving and Gear Shifting all the way.

If you don't believe me, go read the first 12 pages of Quentin Tarantino's *Reservoir Dogs*. It seems to be 'normal', but it isn't. I've even heard some critics claim the opening is both irrelevant and superfluous — but read those pages and go through the Decoding Checklist.

You'll find it's all there. Every single bullet point.

How to fix 'on-the-nose' dialogue? By being oblique. By characters *not* saying what is expected, and *not* revealing what is truly felt.

We've talked at length about Sub-Text — where a character has a sub-textural concern that is hidden behind what is being said out-loud. 'On-the-nose' dialogue has reversed that — it puts the Sub-Text in the character's mouth, instead of behind his eyes. Fix it by putting the sub-text back where it belongs.

(c) SEEK EMOTIONAL TRUTH

Probably the most telling thing that illuminates poor dialogue is most often revealed by Actors when they give you that concerned look and say; '*I don't think my character would say that.'* Nine times out of ten, the thespian is correct. After all, the Actor has worked hard to get under the skin of the character — and probably knows that character better than anyone. As a Director, you need to be as fully aware of the character's background, traits and emotional condition as your Actor. Ideally, you'll have spotted the flaw before it arises on your set — but to do that you may have to read the script multiple times and focus hard on the character's dialogue to determine if a line is 'true' to their personality.

(d) OBSERVE HOW TENSION BUILDS

Watch for how the Writer handles the building of tension in dialogue.

Well-handled conflict tension in dialogue builds slowly. Inexorably. Think about Jack Nicholson's 'Col. Jessup' in Rob Reiner's *A Few Good Men* (Columbia, 1992) written by Aaron Sorkin. 'Jessup' doesn't immediately take the witness stand and yell *'You Can't Handle the Truth!'* The scene builds gradually to that moment. Following that climax, the story tumbles over the edge into its next phase.

Lajos Egri, writing in *The Art of Dramatic Writing* calls this a 'Slowly Rising Tension' — and, boy, does it make for great scenes.

There's an intermediate tension build which, when it works, is incredibly shocking. Egri calls this 'Jumping Tension'. It springs from a motivation that perhaps has not been noticed or which has been sub-texted. A tension will be present, perhaps quite heightened, when very abruptly it explodes — without warning. It's a great tool in horror pictures, and it works well in other genres too. You'll see it in the classic Films Noir quite a lot — an argument gets heated very quickly and suddenly a femme fatale gets slapped.

However, a bad script will have a 'Jumping Tension' that has no foundation — no clear motivation. Someone will start yelling, punching or shooting without a build up, or an underlying reason, that is believable.

Finally, there's tension Lajos Egri describes as 'Static'. There's a big conflict — but nothing happens. The Writer has understood 'conflict' to mean people yelling at each other and mistaken this for drama. The tension doesn't build to a climax that has some kind of 'result'. It's what Shakespeare recognized as something full of 'sound and fury, signifying nothing'.

Watch Martin Scorsese's *Goodfellas* (Warner Bros, 1990) for amazing examples of 'Slowly Rising Tension'.

The *'You think I'm funny?'* scene where Joe Pesci's character 'Tommy DeVito' ratchets the tension on Ray Liotta's 'Henry Hill' is but one of several scenes that exemplify Egri's 'Slowly Rising' definition — and Scorsese's and his cast's immaculate handling of the technique.

(e) BE RUTHLESS WITH CLICHÉ

There are so many clichés prevalent in movies we could make a fun list. Some of it used to be 'hip' — *'You say that like it's a bad thing'.* Some of it has just hung around for decades — *'What seems to be the problem, officer?'* Some of it used to be tough — *'Is that all you got?'*

You get the picture. (Cliché!)

(f) SHOW N'TELL

Writers sometimes prefer to tell. Our job is to show.

We didn't mean to do it! The gun was lying there on the desk when we came in. So, Johnny picked it up. Then we heard something — there was someone in the next room! I wanted to leave, but Johnny said we should take a look — so we did. It was dark, but we could hear somebody moving about....

6. CHARACTER NAMING

Last, and very much least. The Naming of Characters. I find that the same guidelines in respect to originality, tone, heightened effect, 'Special World', 'Theme' and 'Genre' apply in the way writers name their characters. It's a minor point — but significant; illuminating, as always, the quality of the writing.

A couple of examples; Larry Ferguson and Donald Stewart's *The Hunt For Red October* has a character called 'Ramius'. Do you immediately get a sense that the writers want you to feel that this is a protagonist? Is it too much to believe that the word *'ram'* incorporated in the name, with its suggestion of strength and masculinity, was a deliberate and conscious choice? I think not.

How about one of the script's antagonists? 'Ivan Yurievich Putin'. I think it might just have been a coincidence that this bad guy is called 'Putin' but you never know. In any event the name has a wet 'plosive sound to it — like someone spitting. It's close to the word 'puking'. All negative. I'm not being fanciful. These little things matter greatly.

I spoke earlier of John Boorman's 60s noir classic *Point Blank.* Screenwriters Alexander Jacobs & David and Rafe Newhouse adapted Richard Stark's 1962 novel *The Hunter.*

In the novel, the character is called 'Parker' but for *Point Blank*, 'Parker' was changed to 'Walker'. I used to think there were legal or copyright reasons for the change (although I now understand it was because Richard Stark (pseudonym for the great Donald E. Westlake) didn't want an actor closely identified with his multi-book character. Under the continued principle, which my mother taught me, of never allowing the truth to interfere with a good story, I like to think that for the filmmakers there was also a deeper reason for accepting the change — to do with expressing the nature of the character. The name 'Walker' conjures up a simple, straightforward man. It goes further and suggests a man of action. Even further, and it reinforces the principal theme of the film — dogged, focused determination — a man who will keep on being a 'Walker' until he catches up with his enemies and takes his revenge. Further still, once he does catch up with his enemies, circumstances force 'Walker' to do just that — to walk away from the situation, to literally walk away into the darkness, knowing that he will have to keep on going, to walk away from this for the rest of his life.

All that, just from a name. When you think about it, no other name will do. Good screenwriters know this.

They give it to you, the dears.

Final observation on Character Naming. Treat all screenplays that have a character named 'Max' not coupled with the word 'Mad' with great suspicion.

I have no rational explanation for this — other than; (a) In thirty years, I don't think I've ever read a good script with a character called 'Max'; (b) 'Max' is the most popular dog's name in America and writers usually hang out with dogs or cats rather than humans; (c) First time writers zero in on the name 'Max' like heat seeking missiles.

- *Why?*

I have no idea. It's a mystery to me.

And now back to our scheduled program.

CHAPTER THIRTEEN

A Director Reads

The purpose of *The Filmmaker's Art* series is to help you craft a recognizable signature style in a body of work that is unique to you. 'Decoding' a screenplay fluently is a vital first step in developing that skillset.

To become completely at ease with 'Decoding', try to read as many screenplays as you can — both produced and unproduced. Bear in mind that it's just as useful for you to read a "bad" script as it is to read something great.

One of the things you'll often notice when you start to study screenplays — and then see the completed film — is how closely, or not, the director has remained true to the script. (You have to be sure, however, that the script you've studied isn't a Continuity Script that is a word-for-word, shot-by-shot description of an already completed film).

It's useful to notice how directors have deviated from the page. Obviously, producers and marketing divisions have sometimes placed a heavy hand on the footage and crafted the picture the way they wanted. Or perhaps the director shot some of the material present in the script then decided that it didn't move the story forward or obscured the real path (s)he was following. Whatever the case, examine the parts that didn't make it into the final edit and ask yourself 'why'.

Given that you are seeking to develop a unique voice, it makes sense to study a batch of 'produced' screenplays (preferably before you see the film) and determine what *you* take from the Clues presented, and how *you* would shape the film if the script was *yours* to helm. It's a solid exercise in building the muscles of your signature style.

Scripts can be found easily on the open Web, although which version they are is harder to determine. It's a good exercise to find scripts in a variety of different genres, and written at different time periods, then limit your reading to the First Ten Pages of each. Once you've decided the genre(s) you respond to best, then focus in on that genre very completely and study how the genre(s) developed over time. Pay particular attention to contemporary screenplays in the genre, because that's where most conversations are taking place — but make yourself an expert by going into the 'deep cuts' of previous decades.

A screenplay doesn't reveal its Clues in any particular order, so you have to stay alert as they'll start to leap out at you, sometimes when least expected.

In this penultimate chapter, I'm going to round-up the Big Six Primary Clues and go over them briefly one more time. Due to the grey areas of 'Fair Use' copyright law, and the difficulties and time required to deal with studio level legal departments, I've decided to make this wrap-up using unproduced screenplays that I own. The lengthy procedures required to publish large excerpts of produced screenplays — even in what is essentially an academic setting — makes the use of familiar material impractical. However, I encourage you to seek out and read all kinds of scripts, from produced screenplays by A-list writers, to unproduced work by unknown writers. Every script will reveal something important to you.

I'm going to use the following screenplays for this exercise:

- *Cedric's Long Walk*
- *Empire of Blood*
- *In The Deep, Dark Woods*
- *A Dream Into Darkness*

1. GENRE

Generally speaking, Genre is easy to spot. Often from the title alone — as at least two of the above will confirm. A rule of thumb is that if genre seems uncertain, or if it is not apparent early on — then the script is weak. Almost without exception the scripts I'm referencing reveal their genre very quickly and blatantly.

Cedric's Long Walk: (page 2)

```
EXT. NARROW STREET. SKID ROW -- AFTERNOON

Over rooftops and mean streets.  Following an LAPD PATROL
CAR, as it turns into a narrow street of squalid apartment
buildings. There's a CHILD at the far end of the street,
playing with a basketball. He's a little boy. Nine, maybe
ten, years old.  Hair in neat cornrows.  A thin-faced,
solitary kid.  His Mom calls him CEDRIC. He stops bouncing
that ball - and watches warily - as the LAPD PATROL CAR stops
at the curb and two POLICE OFFICERS go into the building.
```

Empire of Blood: (page 4)

```
The roar of the CROWD causes everyone to look down towards
the yet unseen arena.  The noise of the shouts, boos and
jeers seems to intimidate Phaidra.  She's vulnerable, unsure.
Felar's Guests, and passing slaves, block her view. She comes
up the final steps and suddenly there's a gap in front of
her. She has a clear view down into the arena.  What she
sees in monstrous.

A beheaded corpse is sprawled on sand turning crimson.  Six
chained CAPTIVES kneel in a line.  An EXECUTIONER moves behind
them.
```

All of the above is clear and obvious, but not 'Captain Obvious' because this Primary Clue is very much about *you*. It's about identifying genre so you can determine if this is a screenplay that interests you.

Example 1. The LAPD Patrol car, the squalid buildings, the little boy with cornrows — it's a good chance that this is Urban Drama.

Example 2. Roar of the crowd, slaves, a woman called 'Phaedra', an arena where sand is crimson with blood. Right now, this looks like a 'sword n' sandal' saga.

The bottom line for the Genre Clue on your checklist is this. Does the screenplay unfold and fully reveal the Genre Story that the Clue(s) suggest? If not, then you've identified a problem. If so, will you be comfortable and completely awesome working in that genre?

2. THEMATIC STATEMENT

Thematic Statement is hard, and you generally would expect to find several Clues before you could properly formulate it. Because of that, your Statement may not be fully conceived until you're deeper into the script than the First Ten.

The next screenplay example is from *In The Deep, Dark Woods*. Genre was established early on in this screenplay — it's a supernatural horror project, with the added sub-genre of the 'mentally-disturbed-person-who-is-saner-than-everyone-else'. By Page 10, the script has introduced natural elements that have a menacing presence. The woods of the title appear to have an 'evil consciousness'. All well and good, but so far — no 'Thematic Statement' to give the direction a depth that will elevate this particular project into a good, perhaps classic, example of its genre. Then, along comes this scene between NATASHA, the disturbed young woman, and DR. LANDSDOWNE, the controversial quack.

In The Deep Dark Woods: (pages 10,11)

INT. LANDSDOWNE'S OFFICE - MORNING

DR. LANDSDOWNE stands at a french window, looking across the
lawns to the wood. He sips his coffee appreciatively.

>   DR. LANDSDOWNE
>   It's a funny old thing this world,
>   isn't it?

NATASHA stands in the middle of the room. He looks over at
her with a smile.

>   DR. LANDSDOWNE
>   Everyone sees it differently. Some
>   of us agree that what we are seeing
>   is what we are seeing, and some of
>   us don't. You follow? Come over here,
>   a moment. Take a look outside.

Natasha does as instructed, standing by Landsdowne and looking
out at the grounds and the wood beyond.

>   DR. LANDSDOWNE
>   Now, I look out there and I see a
>   beautiful lawn that has been tended
>   carefully for - oh, I don't know - a
>   hundred years. Maybe more. Laid out
>   to give a sense of peace and
>   stability. A view that inspires the
>   mind to relax and to feel secure. A
>   gardener on the other hand, might
>   look out and see endless work. Weeding
>   and mowing and re-sowing. And be
>   worried that winter frost would damage
>   the turf, or careless walkers spoil
>   the surface. What does this view
>   make you feel, Natasha?

In The Deep, Dark Wood 11

Natasha hesitates, sensing a psychological trap.

                    DR. LANDSDOWNE
          Whatever you feel, Natasha. It's
          alright to tell me. There is no wrong
          answer.

Natasha looks out for a long beat. Then at Landsdowne.

                    NATASHA
          Trapped. The lawn makes me feel...it
          makes me feel like a prisoner.

At first glance, this is a very 'normal' scene. A doctor discusses ways of 'seeing', suggesting that different people experience different realities. He links it to a natural element — the lawn. When Natasha looks out, she experiences the reality of the lawn (and the woods beyond) in a completely different way from that of the doctor.

There is something in way this scene has been written that is missing. When the scene begins, we're told that the doctor looks 'across the lawn to the woods'. Then we're told that Natasha looks out 'at the grounds and the woods beyond'. (Yes, the script actually reads 'wood' — singular — in both instances, but that's because it was written in British English not American). Lastly, Natasha looks out for a 'long beat', before telling the doctor she feels 'trapped'.

So, what's missing? From a professional writer's point of view — nothing. Some specific clues have been dropped into the script that will suggest how to shoot and edit this scene. Among those clues are the three plain and neutral descriptions of the POV (point-of-view) shots that two different characters have of the lawn, the grounds, and the woods beyond. At first glance, you might think that they aren't 'clues' at all because there is no indication of how the director should interpret such unassuming descriptions and make the shots. However, interpretation is not a writer's job — although it would have been acceptable to give more of a hint of what the writer imagined. In our example, the important thing the writer has done — and this is why it's a 'clue' — is to keep coming back and referencing the exterior world *from the perspective of both characters*. We don't know how the writer thinks those POV shots of the 'lawn', 'the grounds' or the 'woods beyond' should be presented. Pastoral and pleasant? Gloomy and stark? Detailed and emotive descriptions of the POV shots are not present, but all that means is that *interpretation* is "missing". The task of interpretation has been left entirely to the director. The question that should now arise in any director's mind is;

- *What significance and weight will be given to those particular shots?*

All of us, when we read, see a picture forming in our minds of what is being described. Let's call this an internal 'vision' for want of a better word. Directors are no different from anyone else — they see pictures in their heads when they read. The difference is that directors tend to examine those pictures with a degree of critical analysis. They have to feel that what they see is appropriate. The written word throws up a succession of 'image ideas' and concepts on a director's 'internal movie screen'. These images occur because of interpretation. The difference between what a visual artist, such as a director, "sees" beyond that of the average person is that the artist is exploring the images presented by an *interpretation* of the written word.

If, in reading the script, a director "saw" that Dr. Landsdowne's POV of the lawn and the woods beyond was completely neutral, normal and natural — that would suggest how the shot(s) would be made. That's an 'interpretation' of the written word. Now, given that the scene we're working on is about the ways in which different people experience reality —

indeed, can have their own realities — then a director reading about a disturbed young woman like Natasha will automatically start to consider how she *perceives* things. In this case, and in this genre, Natasha's POV shots would most likely show the lawn and the woods as menacing, distorted and unnatural. Completely opposite to the mundane safe world perceived by Dr. Landsdowne.

This difference would be conveyed to the audience in numerous ways — from lens choices, visual effects, color grading, audio, etc. The goal would be to amplify the *intent* of the scene and make an interpretation that would fit comfortably into the 'Supernatural-Horror-Disturbed-Young-Woman' Genre. With that approach, and that 'vision' and interpretation, a Thematic Statement starts to float up from the depths and become very clear.

- *To Survive, Reality Must Be Questioned and Nature Understood.*

Now, that's a Statement that could prove to be very wrong. I've been able to formulate it here on pages 10 &11, which is reasonably early in my reading of the script. As I continue to read the script, I now have a Thematic Statement that will help me spot if;

(i) reality and natural law begin to distort in ways that will be life-threatening

(ii) the characters start to question their circumstances and perceptions and if

(iii) something nasty happens in the natural world which will have to be understood to be overcome.

If those three conditions continue to be met as the script progresses, then the Thematic Statement will hold. If it "holds" then, for the film to succeed, I will have to "prove" that Survival will require Reality to be questioned and Nature understood. All of which begins to suggest a screenplay with elements that could be traced back to Peter Weir's *Picnic At Hanging Rock* (Atlantic Releasing, 1975) through to a film like James Mangold's *Girl, Interrupted* (Columbia Pictures, 1999). It's a distinguished pedigree and to direct from this script I'd have to be very familiar with that pedigree and stay alert to how the script plays with the genre's standard themes and devices. I'd also need to decide if the screenplay was adding anything fresh to the genre. If not, then a conversation would need to be had with the writer and/or producer.

In our next example, we are at the midpoint of *A Dream Into Darkness*, a Sci-Fi Action Adventure, featuring a protagonist who doesn't seem to know why he's being hunted for a murder he can't remember committing. This is a screenplay that, on the surface, is straight-forward and without any real complexity other than the mystery of '*who-dunnit?*' and the suspense of whether our protagonist, Harry Shaw, can prevail.

- *Searching For The Truth Leads To Great Danger And Unexpected Results.*

Even in the type of action movie we've all seen a million times, there's a need for the director to have a Thematic Statement no matter if it seems, as this one does, rather banal and obvious. The Genre demands excitement, hair-raising moments of danger and the continuing suspense of the protagonist's survival. The Genre demands that Harry Shaw's search for answers should get very interesting indeed.

A Dream into Darkness 47.

As Harry passes by a mirror he stops and studies himself for
a moment, as if he were a stranger.

                    HARRY
               (whispers)
          What am I doing here?

                    LEITH
               (whispers back)
          You think you've got questions!

Leith watches as Harry goes through the room. It's been used
by a woman - clothes have been left behind. Behind a Japanese
screen is a large bed. On a nightstand, a framed photograph.
HARRY picks it up...

INSERT - the photograph. A tall, handsome MAN with his arm
around THERESE. The couple smiling happily for the camera.

                    LEITH (CONT'D)
          Is this your place, Harry?

                    HARRY
          I've never been here before.

                    LEITH
          But you know it. You knew the codes
          to get in. Who's in the photograph?

Harry hands Leith the photograph.

                    LEITH (CONT'D)
          You know who these people are?

                    HARRY
          Do you?

                    LEITH
          Yeah, the man's Patrice Bizou. He
          got taken out by the crew a few years
          back. I don't know the woman.

                    HARRY
          Her name's Therese. They tell me I
          killed her.

                    LEITH
          Did you?

                    HARRY
          If I did, I don't remember.

                    LEITH
          Good defense.

As a filmmaker, I know that to *prove* the two Thematic Statements given above, I have to *show* that Harry Shaw's actions lead to dangerous situations and that every decision brings an unexpected result. I have to *prove* that Natasha's survival depends on questioning reality and finding answers in the natural world.

If Dr. Landsdowne treats Natasha with a new drug that causes her to have pleasant hallucinations, if she wanders into the woods and meets a talking rabbit that explains how Life is, then — amusing as that sounds — the Thematic Statement remains unproven because she's hardly been put in a position where her very survival is at stake.

By the same token, if the script for *A Dream Into Darkness* proceeds to be no more than Harry having some minor brushes with the law, if his actions seldom turn dangerous, and if the answers to his questions turn out to be predictable — then the screenplay is not meeting the requirements that the apparent Thematic Statement is proposing.

Remember that a primary purpose of the Thematic Statement is to help determine if the script is powerful (or not) and has a *direction*. If other issues come up more strongly then the original Statement can always be replaced. But (and I think this is an important 'but') don't forget your initial thematic concept because it will often contain the germ of something that can be used — perhaps in a discovery that will further illuminate character, or in a sub-textural element useful to the development of the story.

Lastly, your Thematic Statement gives you a good Clue as to the size and scope of the screenplay in your hands. How big is the story and its concerns?

Which brings us neatly to...

3. THE STORY ENGINE

A screenplay is a vehicle. You put your actors in the vehicle, start the engine, press on the gas and go on a wild ride.

Although not one of our Primary Six Clues, allow me to say a word about 'Principals' — the lead roles that are an important consideration for The First Ten.

In each of the four screenplays I'm using as examples, the Principals are easy to spot. They're prominent in the First Ten Pages and the stories have their roles at the center.

However, if the characters of Natasha (*In The Deep, Dark Woods*), Harry Shaw (*A Dream Into Darkness*), Cedric Hawkins (*Cedric's Long Walk*) and Phaedra (*Empire of Blood*) turn out to be peripheral, unimportant roles — then you have a really bad screenplay in your hands.

Sometimes a screenwriter may present you with a slight problem and introduce a multitude of characters —an ensemble — so there's no telling who the 'star' is nor which character the story is most about. Except... a good writer kinda does. Although the screenplay might suggest a very strong ensemble cast, you'll notice that one or two roles will dominate. If not — raise an eyebrow.

- *Why, Mr. Innocenti? Surely conventions can be challenged? Do films really have to have only one, maybe two, dominant roles? Why can't a film be made where the ensemble is celebrated, with equal importance being given to each character?*

You might think this is a good idea, comrade, and we'll certainly get the committee to take a look at it. However, there are a number of reasons for 'star' roles. The cynical might suggest these are purely monetary, and it's true that producers, distributors and exhibitors sell and market films because a 'name' brings in the audience (although this is becoming less effective). What is true is that an audience engages more easily, and a story can be more strongly told, if there are dominant characters. How many people identify with Han Solo? How many identify with Luke Skywalker? Katniss Everdeen? Tony Montana? Rocky Balboa? Erin Brockovich? Hermione Granger?

In film storytelling, the audience gets impressed by the spectacle and the spectacular — but is drawn into the story by identifying with, or becoming fascinated by, a specific character. Simple as that.

It's true, of course, that some films are designed for an 'ensemble' cast and that individual characters within the 'ensemble' are treated, or are intended to be treated, as of equal importance. But the storytelling reality is that the audience will have its favorites even if each member of the ensemble is at the top of their game and giving an outstanding performance. It's a quirk of human nature that goes all the way back to the legendary tales that Homer told or the sagas of the Vikings. A primary hero, or heroine, emerges — always — even in stories filled to overflowing with a cast of heroic characters.

Leaving aside the question of Principals — vital though it becomes to our 'vehicle' — our Decoding concern now is with the Story Engine and its main elements; Piston Movement, Gear Shift and the all-important Ignition Event.

IGNITION EVENT

Do the screenplays we're examining all have Ignition Events? Yes.

- *Empire of Blood* has Phaedra witness the execution of rebel slaves and watch a gladiatorial combat for the first time. It's a sequence that bloodily throws us into the ancient world she belongs to.

- *Cedric's Long Walk* has a little boy witness the police arrest his mother's violent boyfriend for domestic abuse. The consequences of that arrest play out in tragic ways before 'order' is restored.

- *A Dream Into Darkness* has Harry Shaw arrested for a murder he did not commit. The whole screenplay is about what actually happened — and why.

- *In The Deep, Dark Woods* has runaway Natasha brought back to an institution she has previously escaped from — an 'Ignition' which turns out to be as much a conclusion as a beginning.

You'll sometimes come across scripts that don't have obvious Ignition Events. There are some great movies out there where Ignition takes place off-screen, or in the past. As long as there is something that pushes the story into being — giving it a beginning that can be pointed to — that's all that matters.

What you must be careful of is the Ignition that is too big for the story that follows and which (although this is an issue of personal taste) bears no connection or real relevance to the story that is about to unfold. Those Ignition events are usually there to (a) grab attention away from the popcorn and (b) allow the protagonist to look cool — the cringe-worthy technique of so many 80s films that now appear so dated.

PISTON MOVEMENT & GEAR SHIFTS

If you look at some of Mr. Tarantino's writing — I'm thinking of *Reservoir Dogs* (Miramax, 1992) and *Inglourious Basterds* (Universal/ Weinstein, 2009) in particular — you'll find lengthy opening scenes where a slow swing of the pendulum

somehow, almost hypnotically, draws us close to his characters. The completion of the scenes are Piston Movements in
themselves — true — but his long dialogue scenes are more
about Gear Shifting, sometimes with a noisy and grating transmission, other times as smooth as silk.

There are some people who do not believe that lengthy
conversational dialogue (or, heaven forbid, monologue) is interesting, dramatic, or fulfills the requirements of the Story Engine.

That viewpoint is correct if the dialogue in question is
poorly crafted and is filling pages with no particular place to
go. But dialogue that is full of disagreements, non sequiturs,
bantering argument and clashing viewpoints, or of slowly revealed tension and discordant sub-texts is another matter entirely. Just ask Mr. Tarantino. The reason lengthy dialogue
scenes can work is because — written correctly — they're just
brimming with Gear Shifts.

Once identified, the Gear Shift Clue is there to allow you
to ask yourself how each actor should deliver the lines and
what should be the correct amount of menace/jocularity/bewil-
derment etc., that *you* feel ought to be expressed.

This is 'ground zero' for your direction, the point where
you start to see how to shape the performances. It is also a
moment to ask yourself how the off-the-page characters are
reacting in the scene, because their behaviors — boredom,
amusement, engagement, impatience — hold the potential for
interesting Gear Shifts when it's time to film. Let's look at a
few;

In The Deep, Dark Woods: (page 4):

Rhonda reaches across the table and taps Natasha's forehead
with her spoon.

> RHONDA
> We're talking to you, dummy!

Everyone laughs at Natasha's surprised expression. Only LAURA
seems concerned.

> LAURA
> That's not nice, Rhonda!

> RHONDA
> What the fuck do you care, Laura?

> LAURA
> Just saying. Maybe she's scared.
> First time and all... I was scared...

> RHONDA
> That's because you're a pathetic
> bitch.
> (to Natasha)
> Are you scared, sweetheart?

There's no reaction from Natasha, who goes back to her soup -
and then turns her placid gaze back onto the staff table.

> RHONDA (CONT'D)
> Man, I wish they'd give me the shit
> they're giving her. Whatever it is.

Two interesting Gear Shifts in this *Dark Woods* scene. Three, if
you count Natasha's surprise at being hit with a spoon, and
then her lapse back into semi-catatonia. Rhonda's level of aggression has four distinct parts — the first when she's address-
ing Natasha, and the second when she turns on Laura. The
third and fourth parts are the wheedling *'Are you scared,
sweetheart?'* followed by the 'I-give-up' tone of her final line.

If we count Rhonda as a single strand of quick Gear
Shifting, then the second Gear Shift is Laura. She intervenes —

there's a personal strength in her *'That's not nice, Rhonda!'* as she takes the moral high ground — but Rhonda turns on the aggression and Laura makes a Gear Shift. *'Just saying. Maybe she's scared.'*

Laura's not strong enough to back Rhonda down, and she knows it. It's not as obvious a Gear Shift Clue as those given for Rhonda — but the hesitancy of her last line and her silence thereafter are suggestive.

If I were to tell you that Laura commits suicide about ten pages further on, this scene would be a key moment to re-read and examine. You have to ask yourself if this is the moment that sends Laura over the edge. A Gear Shift, with a massive consequence, being processed internally in Laura's thoughts? If so, how will you film it?

The Writer has the scene end on Rhonda 's line. There's no action/description that brings us back to Laura. You could cut with the final shot of Rhonda and nobody would think there was anything missing. You'd have 'shot the script'. No Director ever got fired for that.

Alternatively, there is a hint, given Rhonda 's reference to Natasha's medication, to end the scene on Natasha mechanically eating her soup. After all, the scene has been largely about the dynamic that exists in the group now that Natasha has become part of it, and about how Natasha is in a zombie-like state. In fact, as the scene begins with Natasha being tapped on the forehead with a spoon, it might be nice and tidy to end the scene (to 'bookend') by going back to Natasha and have her — only now — rub her forehead... conveying further the slowed-down, catatonic state she's in. But, there's that darn Laura Clue — which now starts to hammer insistently at us because in ten pages Laura's going to commit suicide.

So, do you deal with that? Does the scene end not on Rhonda or Natasha, but on Laura? Do you make a lingering shot of Laura and allow the audience to see the effect Rhonda 's bullying has had, and 'see' the Gear Shift which foreshadows suicide?

Those are just three ways that you might come out of the scene — but there's sure to be others. This single Clue of Laura's Gear Shift compels you to examine how you will interpret and proceed. You are being forced to make a selection from multiple possibilities and now have to ask yourself what you will discard, and what you will keep.

What follows is a sequence in two scenes from early in *Cedric's Long Walk*.

The first scene in the sequence has the little boy realize that the removal of Mom's boyfriend hasn't made her happy. If he was expecting Rolanda to say; *'we're all good now that my abusive boyfriend has been arrested. How about I make some cookies?'* he is going to be sorely disappointed. The scene is an example of a minor Piston Movement, in this instance conveyed through the unspoken Gear Shift performed by a child actor. Remember the importance of the polarities that make a scene both interesting and necessary? Hot to Cold? Red to Green? This is a scene where the expectation of one of the characters gets shifted. From 'Happy-Solution-Of-A-Problem' to 'Confused Disappointment'.

```
INT. KITCHEN. TENEMENT APARTMENT -- DAY

CEDRIC finds ROLANDA at the sink.  She dabs at her bruised
face with a wet dishcloth.

                        CEDRIC
            Mom?

Rolanda looks around.  She seems exhausted and worn.

                        CEDRIC (CONT'D)
            Are you okay?

She nods, and turns away.  Running cold water over the
dishcloth and wringing it out.  Cedric reaches up to touch
her arm.

                        CEDRIC (CONT'D)
            Mom?

He waits until she looks down at him.

                        CEDRIC (CONT'D)
            It's lucky.

                    ROLANDA
            What are you talking about?

                        CEDRIC
            It's lucky.  That the cops took Luis
            away.

                    ROLANDA
            Lucky?

                        CEDRIC
            Luis might have hurt you. You were
            lucky the cops came.

                    ROLANDA
            You listen, Cedric.  Cops are always
            bad luck!  Understand?  Whoever called
            them didn't do us any favors!

Cedric is crest-fallen.  Rolanda leaves the room.
```

The second scene in the sequence — Mom realizing that it was Cedric, (not the nosy neighbor) who called the police — ends with a distinct and unexpected Gear Shift, but this time from Mom. But before we get to that, the second scene first amplifies the Gear Shift Cedric experienced in the previous scene — a disappointment that made him retreat to his room and his coloring book.

```
INT. CEDRIC'S BEDROOM. TENEMENT APARTMENT -- LATER

A tiny, box-like room.  CEDRIC sits on his bed.  Upset.
Half-heartedly doodling in a coloring book.  The door opens.
ROLANDA stares in at him.

                    ROLANDA
          Did you call them, Cedric?
```

WHITE Revision - 5-2-07   6.

```
Cedric doesn't respond.  He looks down at his coloring book.

                    ROLANDA (CONT'D)
          You look at me when I'm talking to
          you!  Did you call them?!

                    CEDRIC
          No.

His answer infuriates her.  She snatches his arm and hauls
him to his feet.

                    ROLANDA
          You're lying through your mouth,
          boy!
               (shaking him)
          You tell me the truth!  Did you call
          the police?  Did you call them?!
          You answer me!

                    CEDRIC
               (wails, tearful)
          He was hurting you, Mama!  He's always
          hurting you!  I hate him.  I don't
          want him with us!  We've got to get
          away from him!

                    ROLANDA
          Where, Cedric?  Where are we going
          to go!?  You tell me where we're
          going to go!

                    CEDRIC
          Long Reach!  We could go live in
          Long Reach!!

Rolanda suddenly bursts out laughing and lets Cedric go.
```

Now, when Mom seems to be at her angriest, Cedric has to go from denial to pleading his case. It's a switch from a negative position to one where he suggests another positive solution to their problems. But Cedric gets the name of the city wrong (he says; 'Long Reach' not 'Long Beach') — and that

makes Mom 'gear shift' from anger to laughter. Maybe she'll make cookies after all!
It will be interesting to see how the actress playing Rolanda will make that shift. How do you see it? If the actress chooses something that doesn't have the 'moment' you're looking for — how do you help her bring it?

We've previously learned that Piston Movement is big stuff, and largely a mechanical motion as the story turns and develops. Clearly, you have to be aware of its presence or absence or if there's a minor Piston Movement in the shape of the Gear Shift that will drive the story forward. For me, so much of directing is in the Gear Shift — which is why I focus on it here.

The second 'Cedric' scene above has those distinct but minor Piston Movements — in the mother's angry realization and in Cedric's upset and pleading. The mother's laughter at the end of the scene is the final 'beat' of those Piston Movements. You could direct the scene without any further information. Angry Mom. Upset Child. Angrier Mom. Feisty Child. Even Angrier Mom. Desperately-Seeking-Solution Child. Amused & Anger-Dissolving Mom.

But to go through the scene like that is just listening to the Engine moving. You're still sitting in the garage. The scene will be present on your editor's hard drive but it's unlikely that there will be a performance captured that will move your audience.

- *Why?*

Because you haven't turned up the volume, you haven't lowered the flame, you haven't steered a path, or slowed for a turn in the road. You've merely observed the motions of the Piston. Without controlling the Gear Shifting that causes the movement, your direction will become passive. It will be a series of checkpoints. Was the Mom angry? Check. Was the child upset? Check.

Management of the Gear Shift is key to; (i) a performance that will draw your audience in, (ii) contriving a movie experience that elicits an emotional response and (iii) showing the audience who your characters really are.

Your job — and, trust me, not all Directors do this — but your job is (i) to see where those Gear Shifts are, (ii) have a clear idea in your head how you hear and see those Shifts and (iii) know exactly where they should be going.

Once on set or location, watch and listen to how your Actors are moving through the Gear Shifts and then (i) either accept with dumb amazement and gratitude how wonderfully they have understood and presented those moments or (ii) guide them to an interpretation that works.

4. SUB-TEXT

Sometimes, even in amazingly great scripts, you don't find much Sub-Text — particularly in the First Ten. That's not necessarily a bad thing. The absence of specific Sub-Text Clues doesn't mean the script is poor, it just means that the Actors — and you, the Director — may find it appropriate to add some. When you read the script try to have one part of your brain registering if there's a Sub-Text Clue present or not, and — if not — ask yourself what that Sub-Text might be if it turns out to be needed. That way you're prepared when Actors are in the vicinity and searching for their characters.

Constructing a little 'sub-textural back-story' is a useful tool. Now, when I talk about 'back-story' it sounds a little precious. Even to me. There are plenty of Actors who delight in building a complete biography for their character so that they can fill out their performance. All Actors do this to a degree. But often, pressure of time, heat of the moment, last minute re-write of the script, change in tone — any number of reasons — can throw the Actor a curveball and suddenly there's no sub-textural anchor to hold onto.

At other times, (and this happens more often) the Writer hasn't provided a sub-text because the scene or dialogue in question is straight-forward and clear. Adding a layer of Sub-Text becomes irrelevant and annoying.

But while 'backstory' and other 'sub-textural' suggestions can get too complex and there's a danger of just sounding silly and pretentious on-set, you can run into trouble if you're unprepared for all eventualities.

If a script doesn't have an obvious Sub-Text Clue, or doesn't seem to require Sub-Text, don't imagine that you will never need to dig it out and present it to the Actors. You don't want to be left without a Sub-Textural response when it's being requested or if it's the only way to get the performance to the optimum level.

When you read a scene, pay attention as to the *possible* Sub-Text in every line that's delivered, and, where Sub-Text has been presented by the Writer, run it through your story filter and Thematic Statement to make sure it's going to work.

Here's a scene/sequence from *A Dream Into Darkness* (two separate locations/times of day) that has very obvious sub-textural elements going on.

The writer has indicated these clearly, but — as the Director — you will have to watch how the two Actors approach what is going on 'inside' their heads and the sub-texts which are acknowledged but not spoken;

INT. COMMANDER'S OFFICE - POLICE HQ - NIGHT

               MORNINGSIDE
          (on monitor, smiles)
      I hope this conversation is private?

             COMMANDER DURACK
      I guarantee it. Although I should
      tell you that all conversations I
      have in this office are "archived".

               MORNINGSIDE
      It's important to me that my partners
      on Kanal are not disturbed
      unnecessarily by anything we might
      discuss.

INT. MORNINGSIDE'S OFFICE - MAGIC

MORNINGSIDE watches the effect his words have on DURACK.

             COMMANDER DURACK
          (on monitor, carefully)
      Well, that would depend on the
      situation.

                      Filmworks, U.S.A. L.L.C.

                   A Dream into Darkness 9.

               MORNINGSIDE
      I have an internal problem that need
      not be of any concern to my partners.
      I would very much like it to be
      handled by just the two of us.
      Confidentially.

INT. COMMANDER'S OFFICE - POLICE HQ - NIGHT

DURACK closely watches Morningside's face.

             COMMANDER DURACK
      I don't see why not, Jerome. As long
      as you remember that one hand washes
      the other.

On the monitor, Morningside acknowledges with a smile, then
becomes serious.

               MORNINGSIDE
      Something bad, very bad, happened
      here a few days ago, Commander. I've
      just learned that the man responsible
      has arrived on Kanal. His name is
      Harry Shaw.

5. TEXTURE

Here's some examples from the four screenplays:

In The Deep, Dark Woods (page 2):

```
EXT. EDGE OF THE WOOD - EVENING

We are moving through an ancient wood. Trees covered with
moss and creepers, the woodland floor thick with decomposed
vegetation and twisted roots.  A brooding stillness amongst
the trees.  Then comes the SOUND of a cold wind, an icy breath
that shakes the treetops.
```

This is the moment when the Dark Woods of the title is first established. This isn't a place where bunnies run around in sunlit glades and fawns stop to drink at bubbling brooks. Look at the words — 'ancient', 'creepers', 'decomposed', 'twisted', 'brooding'. Then along comes an audio texture — the 'icy breath that shakes the treetops.' Put a frame around it and you're done.

Cedric's Long Walk (page 2):

```
STORAGE ROOM OFF LANDING -- Light filters through a broken,
grimy window and into a tiny room filled with junk.  CEDRIC
keeps the broken door open a crack, and watches as the POLICE
OFFICERS drag LUIS out of the apartment in handcuffs.  LUIS
curses AD LIB in Spanish and spits at ROLANDA.  She wails,
and feebly tries to stop the arrest.

                    ROLANDA (CONT'D)
          He didn't mean it!  Don't take him!
          Please don't take him!
```

This example from urban drama *Cedric's Long Walk* is set in the kind of minor location that you're constantly pre-sented with as a filmmaker. The important action is the child's POV of the cops on the stairs — which means that this small 'set' may ultimately not even exist on the actual location but will have to be either built or shot in another place and then cut into the film to make it appear that it *is* part of the location.

Given that this could end up being a studio-built set, the Texture Clues are very important if you want to convey a continuity of space.

The Texture Clues given concern both Art Dept., and Lighting Dept. The little room is lit with daylight which '*filters through*' a '*cracked, grimy window*'. Then we're given the Clue to the contents of the room. '*Junk*'.

Not much in the way of Clues— some questions to ask yourself might be: '*What kind of junk? What does the light look like? Is there dust in the air? Are there cobwebs on the window?*'

A Dream Into Darkness (page 3):

```
I/E BUBBLECAB - TRAVELING - NIGHT

A small capsule with a NAVIGATOR up front and room for two
passengers to squeeze in back. Between the Navigator's knees -
a guidance display and control stick. The cab's domed canopy
is heavily scratched, so visibility is poor. Strips of light
whizz by. HARRY settles back as the cab picks up speed, moving
up a steep incline.
```

This example from sci-fi screenplay *A Dream Into Darkness* demonstrates that Texture can be indicated to reinforce the way the genre is to be presented, and to assist in getting a 'Look'.

In this case, 'heavily scratched' canopy and 'room for two passengers to squeeze in' are two Clues which tell us that, in this hi-tech world, objects get used and life is not entirely comfortable. We're not in bright, shiny, endlessly spacious sci-fi world — we're in cramped, claustrophobic, well-used sci-fi universe.

The scratched canopy also allows us to be vague about the exterior view from the 'bubblecab' and create Texture (and movement) from light sources.

Empire of Blood (page 10):

```
ON THE ARENA FLOOR

Here, the noise and color of the CROWD is muted - but the
smallest details of gladiatorial combat are terrifyingly
loud, clear and sharp.  Metal clashes against metal.  Leather
creaks as muscular bodies strain and twist.  Each parry,
each thrust, is accompanied by grunts, gasps and labored
breaths.  Sweat stains fabric, and runs freely down arms,
chests, legs.  Quint's OPPONENT, tiring from his early
frenzied assault, becomes ever more desperate.  He flails at
Quint, drawing blood in a long wound before Quint can lean
away from the blow.  The CROWD rises, baying for death.
```

Some interesting Texture Clues here, most of them for the Costume, Props and Make-Up Departments.

Sound is being used as a texture too — the 'muted' noise and color of the Crowd, the 'metal clashes' and 'leather creaks'. The writer is suggesting that the foreground action should really pop out from the background. As the Director, I might agree!

The above scene description from *Empire of Blood* is part of a three-minute sequence of bloody and violent action staged under intense sunlight. A harsh, unforgiving environment filled with terror and mayhem.

And then the script abruptly cuts to...

```
EXT. THE DECRAS ESTATE/GARDENS & PATIOS -- MAGIC

In the exquisite gardens, built on a hillside overlooking
the capital, a party is underway.  Banquet tables are laid
out by fountains, arbors and lawns.  The ELITE mingle and
gossip.  SLAVES, constantly attentive, bear trays with unusual
delicacies.  PHAIDRA moves amongst her GUESTS.  Young CALOT,
in more formal attire than he wore at the Arena, covertly
follows her progress, catching snippets of conversation.

                    MATRONLY GUEST
          I've looked everywhere for General
          Felar...

                    PHAIDRA
          He's promised to be here - but he's
          dining first with the Emperor...

FURTHER ON

                    POMPOUS ELDER MAN
               (slurping oysters)
          Marriage agrees with you, young lady,
          you're blooming!
```

These two excerpts from gladiatorial epic *Empire of Blood* follow on from one another and demonstrate how Texture can sometimes have an element of Piston Movement. It's a big dramatic swing of the pendulum to go from the sweat, leather and metal textures of mortal combat to banquet tables laid out by fountains, and slaves bearing trays of unusual delicacies.

In both sequences, the demands of Texture are enormous. In reading the script, you would have to have an awareness of how that level of textural detail could be accomplished — or even if it should be attempted. Matters of budget, crewing, casting, costuming, weapons training, location, atmospheric personnel (extras!), stunt work, ambitious production design and cinematography come to the fore. How much do you and your producers care? How much can you afford to care? Do you hold out for a fight coordinator like the late great William Hobbs so that you can get gladiatorial swordplay both authentic and thrilling? Who can get the costuming right — but not make it appear tired and overly familiar? Will the crowds be computer-generated, or will you be in some far-flung location where you can fill those arena seats with correctly costumed extras? And if you can, how many Assistant Directors are going to be required to control that crowd? How much of the detail matters to you and your producers? I can guarantee that there will be a question about the oysters being slurped by POMP-OUS ELDER MAN. Do they really have to be oysters? And what about the other foods being served at the garden party? Maybe you think it will be acceptable to put a variety of snacks from a convenience store on the trays. Nobody will notice, right?

But while some Directors won't care too much about the delicacies on those trays, others — Maestro Fellini, for example — would make sure that what the audience saw would cause wonder, amazement, amusement and, more than likely, revulsion. Directing always comes down to the details. If it's in the frame — it's important. The buttons on an actor's costume. The shade of red on the lady's lips. The oyster being popped into the mouth of the character actor.

I don't want to draw too much attention to the quality of the writing in these 'Texture' examples. It's good enough, but you'll find better — and worse. What I *do* want to point out is that it's not helpful when writers don't give you some Textural Clue and, to me, that points to poor writing overall. When you have been given Texture Clues, treat them with respect — unless they don't fit into your vision of how the Genre should be approached.

6. IMAGE AND AURAL SYSTEMS

The Clues for building an image an/or aural system are probably not going to be apparent in the First Ten Pages, and may not be presented consciously by the screenwriter at all. However, your reading may suggest a System even when nothing has been placed into the script deliberately.

EXT. DESERTED STREETS. COMPTON -- EARLY MORNING

SERIES OF SHOTS -- **CEDRIC** walks down strangely quiet streets.
As he crosses over an intersection he HEARS an engine. A
block away. A black HUMMER **H2** slowly passes and disappears.

WHITE Revision - 5-2-07   66.

The streets are narrow. Cedric comes to a T-junction, the
way ahead blocked by tin walls covered in graffiti. Looking
back he gets a glimpse of the same prowling Hummer.

FURTHER ON -- CEDRIC looks up and sees a JETLINER descending.
It's going the same way he is. He turns left to go south.
Ahead, he sees the black Hummer cross over, east to west.

FURTHER ON -- A wider intersection. Cedric reaches the far
south east corner and trots on. Behind him, the Hummer
appears, bass end kicking on the sound system. It passes
by, does a u-turn, comes back and stops. Cedric slows as he
approaches the parked vehicle. He glances around. Sees
nobody. He can't see through the tinted glass into the H2.

The electric purr of the passenger window. Smoke curls out.

                    SLIP
          Hey, little bro'.

Cedric stops. He sees **SLIP**, 32. Slip has a lean, feral
look. A smile lacking warmth. Cedric glances at **BONE**, 28,
the driver - a thug, pure and simple.

                    SLIP (CONT'D)
          You seen a red Camaro roun' here?

                    CEDRIC
          No.

                    SLIP
          You know what a Camaro looks like?

                    CEDRIC
          I ain't seen nothing.

The story of urban drama *Cedric's Long Walk* concerns a little boy who, after his mother's death, makes a hazardous journey from L.A. to Long Beach. Here on Page 65/66 he is heading south through Compton, CA in the early morning. He's been told, in a previous scene, that if the big commercial 'planes are descending into LAX they're heading west — and he must head south.

Yes, it took me to Page 66, but I suddenly realized that the 'Jetliner descending' and 'bass-end kicking on the sound system' were my (Aural) System triggers. Given that the little boy travels through a myriad of Los Angeles' districts, I realized that each neighborhood has its own 'aural flavor' and that to deliberately recognize and introduce a specific sound signature for each milestone on the journey, in ways that were not obvious, would give the film an interesting cohesion. So, I went back and started to find those moments.

That's the beginning of an Aural System, but what about the Image System for this screenplay? The story arcs from a very dark place (Skid Row, Los Angeles and the murder of Rolanda, Cedric's mother) to the sunlit shores of Long Beach and the child being reunited with family. The story arc would suggest the 'Look' of the film slowly changing from a monochromatic, blue-grey scale to full color — in much the same way that many of the classic film noir stories of the 1940s tended to begin in nighttime darkness and end at dawn with the sun coming up to chase away the shadows.

But, a 'Look' is *not* an 'Image System'.

Because this screenplay is about a solitary journey made by a little boy, the most obvious Image System might well be that the 'world' of the film is seen from a child's viewpoint. It's an Image System that would have adults looming over the child, creating a very oppressive feeling. The angle of each shot would then have to conform to an Image System that expressed what the child was feeling in terms of his personal space, his sense of security or his lack of familiarity. That's fairly bold and interesting, I think you'll agree.

An alternative Image System could reinforce the child's sense of confusion and anxiety at being lost and alone by using physical locations that seem to take him further away, and deeper into, worlds he doesn't know or understand. Subway tunnels. Descending steps. Wide, vacant lots that seem like alien wastelands. Vistas where perspective is warped. Places where people and objects are too bright, too fast, too busy, too confusing.

Hey, can't we have both? But, of course!

Empire of Blood

An 'Image System' for gladiator epic *Empire of Blood*? I'm thinking 'birds'. The ancient world was filled with omens and superstitions. First, I'd do the research as to how ancient civilizations regarded specific birds. Next, I'd have to be very careful that my avian Image System didn't become a 'Symbol'. Which means I'd have to be subtle and not put a crow in the foreground of a shot to evoke 'menace' or be a harbinger of death. I'd take a more naturalistic approach, couple it with an Aural System (fluttering wings, birdsong, etc.,) and consider putting Image System elements — almost unnoticeably —into costuming, set dressing, props and set decorating.

I stress *almost unnoticeably*. Once an Image System becomes too integrated into over-all production design it rapidly becomes obvious and loses its power. It may be a cohesive, unifying and visually satisfying element in the film — but it is now a 'Design' and is no longer playing on subliminal feelings and emotions. The 'bird' Image System I'm suggesting for *Empire of Blood* would have to be subtle. I'd probably not wish to use it for a single conceptual purpose, but perhaps use in contrasting ways and help underline not just Power and State Authority, but also elements of Gentleness, Love and the desire for Freedom.

A Dream Into Darkness

A sci-fi script set on a wintry artificial satellite where it is permanently night?

I'd probably go elemental and use water as the Image System. Water in all its forms — from ice to steam. That gives me huge potential to incorporate my Image System into Texture.

Doing so would be a good example of the 'specialized' form of Texture I mentioned earlier where the Image System is a deliberately imposed layer which adds a psychological element into Texture.

A broad example might be this: The screenplay has many scenes where things are not working out for Harry Shaw, the protagonist. Scenes where he can't get the answers fast enough. Scenes where obstacles impede his progress or reverse his efforts. If those scenes had within them Textural elements brought into the filming in such a way as to heighten his frustration — then that becomes an Image System. Frost makes it hard to open a door or see through the domed canopy of the Bubblecab. Ice makes him slip all the way down a ramp. Deep snow makes it hard to walk fast enough to keep up with someone he's tailing.

At the other extreme, actions that are fast and definitive may keep occurring in the presence of swift-running water, or steam.

In this way, not only are the required Textural elements present — they are being manipulated by the Director to deepen psychological responses.

The trick is to have the Image System present but in ways that the audience is not consciously aware of.

In The Deep, Dark Woods: (page 7)

```
EXT. PLAYING FIELD & GARDEN - MORNING

A volleyball game in progress, watched by PATIENTS and STAFF
with KIM in one of the teams.  NATASHA wanders on the fringe
of the onlookers and drifts away.  She passes through an
iron gate...

... and into a walled garden. She passes a greenhouse where
PATIENTS are busy tending plants.  She continues down a path,
under a trellis.  LAURA sits on a bench by a sundial, writing
in a journal.  Natasha stops when she sees her, and is about
to retreat - but Laura looks up.

                    LAURA
          It's okay.

                    NATASHA
          Sorry.

Natasha walks up to the sundial, hesitant and unable to look
at Laura. Laura studies her.  Natasha doesn't know how to
start a conversation so finds the sundial more interesting.
There's some lettering etched into the brass face.

                    LAURA
          Tempus fugit

                    NATASHA
          What?

                    LAURA
          On the sundial.  It's Latin.

                    NATASHA
          Oh. What does it mean?

                    LAURA
          Time flies.  Which is ironic really.
               (off Natasha's
               puzzlement)
          Because it doesn't. Not here.
```

Well, that's nice. Right there on Page 7. A sundial. Time
flies. Or doesn't. I'd be looking to build an Image System
through the use of Time. Clocks. Lengthening shadows. Day

into Night. Jarring 'Time Cuts' in the edit. Camera motion that allows actors to be in one place at one moment, and in an unexpectedly different place a few seconds later. I'd be seeking to play with Time, and our perception of the passage of Time. I'd be relentless about it, and probably throw in an Aural System with clock movement, chimes, perhaps some kind of metronomic sound design that gives a mechanical counterpoint to the other major element present in the screenplay; Nature.

Thanks for staying with me through this wrap-up and review. We've been through the Big Six Clues, and I threw in a note about Principal Players (a First Ten "must-have") in the Story Engine section.

To complete everything you will need to fully decode the First Ten Pages and more (not forgetting the Captain Obvious Clues) let me conclude this chapter with a final word about...

THE SPECIAL WORLD

This Clue, you'll recall, is not part of the Big Six, but was added into our discussion of the First Ten. If you were to ask me for the Clue that interests me most about any screenplay — leaving aside Genre, because there are only a few genres I feel comfortable with — then I'd probably point to The Special World.

Every song can be interpreted, every book can be adapted, every ballet can be danced, and every screenplay can be realized in entirely different ways by the interpretive artists who approach the original work.

In film, the interpretive artist is the Director.

What does this mean? It means a huge responsibility. The manner in which you interpret and realize the screenplay will be unique to you. Another Director would have done

everything differently. Everything. This is why studios and producers and international movie stars pay such close attention
to the person they bring onboard to interpret the script.

Generally speaking, it's not the way you interpret the
lines of dialogue, choreograph the action, or suggest the sub-
text that is truly important. The thing that engages audiences
and producers most is how the Special World is presented.

The Special World is arrived at through a director interpreting a screenplay and building a 'vision' for the film. Person-
ally, I dislike the word 'vision'. It implies that a director is not
quite human, that he or she is a person endowed with god-like
powers that other beings cannot hope to possess.

Nonsense. 'Vision' is nothing more than having a very
clear idea — and perhaps an-almost-original idea — of how a
Special World should be presented. The more 'avant-garde',
extra-ordinary or just plain 'weird' the clear idea is, the more
that director will be described as 'visionary'. Another word I try
not to think about when having lunch.

It is necessary for you to have that clear idea. The
writer, we hope, has aided you greatly in this regard. If not,
then you have to think carefully, go back over the various ways
the genre has built the Special World in the past, think of directions that the genre might now follow.

Noir-ish crime thrillers set in Los Angeles give way to
noir-ish crime thrillers set in Oslo. Sci-fi films set in dark, post-
apocalyptic cities teeming with multi-racial hordes give way to
sci-fi films set on distant planets with pristine high technology
and an almost total absence of human life. The Genres are
fixed. Special Worlds evolve.

I'm discussing 'vision'. Much as I dislike the word. I'm
not talking about the physical creation of the Special World.
That belongs to a Director's collaborators who 'own' so much
of the film, and who have contributed endlessly and tirelessly

to the finished product. Your Production Designer and Key Department Heads bring the Special World alive — but the 'vision' for that Special World is the interpretation that the
Director takes from the script and then distributes amongst
cast and crew. It's about guidance. It's about knowing what is
right and appropriate and true — and being able to dismiss
everything that does not meet the criteria of the vision formulated from your reading of the script.

Very often, the Director 'gets' what the writer has given
him so completely that he is able to create a Special World that
is true in every detail to what the writer imagined and goes
even further to create aspects of the World that did not form
part of the Writer's concept, but which are entirely consistent
and authentic. That's great interpretation. Sadly, the opposite
frequently happens and what might have been a fascinating
Special World on the page, turns out to be rather less satisfac-
tory on screen.

My belief is that the difference between being an 'acceptable' Director and being a 'great' Director is, for the most
part, dependent on how well the Director creates a Special
World — no matter how thinly (or poorly) it might have been
present in the script. The same is true for all interpretive artists.
Give a good and 'acceptable' actor a line of mediocre dialogue
and it'll come out alright, for the most part. Give the same line
to a truly great actor and it will be interpreted in a way that will
make it shine.

There's a saying quite often heard in the film world. A
good film has two great scenes — and no bad ones. I think
that's a guideline not just for films, but for how we can broadly
differentiate between poor, average, good and great interpretive skills. To become a truly fine interpretive artist, you need to
be strong in all areas. But you need to be great in two. And one
of those should be in how you see, build and control the Special World of the films you will make.

CHAPTER FOURTEEN

The Captain's Farewell

I hope these pages have given you an understanding that an informed reading of a screenplay sets you up for success and gives you advance warning of the potential for failure.

In many respects, you're very much alone when you work as a Director. You have to protect yourself — and the project — not only in terms of your creativity and personal vision, but also from a quagmire of bad choices resulting from the ambitious expectations of others.

Writers have the luxury of satisfying their creativity from the comfort of a chair in a quiet room, most often without a deadline. You don't. You have to translate those words into pictures, in ways that will astonish and amaze. You have to do it under pressure, with budget limitations, with unreasonable time demands, with worried people in expensive suits looking over your shoulder, with fractious artists displaying moods and insecurities, with exhausted technicians who look to you for energy and leadership.

You should think about those things when you read the script. Seek out the 'Captain Obvious Clues' and ask yourself; *How do I do this? How do I bring this project in on time and on budget?* The answers you give yourself, or the doubts raised, will lead to positive conversations with smart, professional producers and more difficult discussions with the less-experienced and the over-optimistic. But you need to have the conversations so that you don't get set up for failure.

Lastly, consider what you've read and learned in *Decoding The Script* as a means to focus yourself and your career. You're going to find scripts. Some will be the perfect vehicle to push you forward. Others will stall or delay you. It's important to be able to make the distinction between them.

In my own career, I have been attached to direct over twenty pictures. Four of them have been produced. A hit rate that low isn't unusual, but is entirely due to becoming attached to too many projects that were not fully developed, were too expensive to make, were not appealing to the marketplace due to elements of Genre or Theme, and which didn't have sufficient depth (Story, Structure, Sub-Text, Texture) or immediate surface appeal (Casting, Locations, Dialogue, Production Values) to make them viable.

Being attached to those projects wasted my time and my energy. They certainly helped me develop skills and sharpen my judgment, but they got me stuck for months — if not years — at a time when I could have been moving forward and allowing other doors to open. I've written this book to help you avoid that — and to remind myself not to get stuck again.

It is time now to bid you *'au revoir'* as this concludes the first volume of *The Filmmaker's Art*.

You'll have noticed that, under the 'Captain Obvious Clues', the only item on the list not discussed was Pace & Rhythm. It's not an oversight, because the topic belongs either in Structure & Form as we've already seen, or in matters to do with Performance and Editing which we haven't reached yet. That's a coming attraction. As far as a 'Captain Obvious' bullet point goes, it's there to remind you that Pace & Rhythm is yet another issue that causes concern amongst those who will first read the script.

You'll have an answer in any case, because you have mastered the concept of the 'Goldberg Variation' - and they haven't!

ABOUT THE AUTHOR

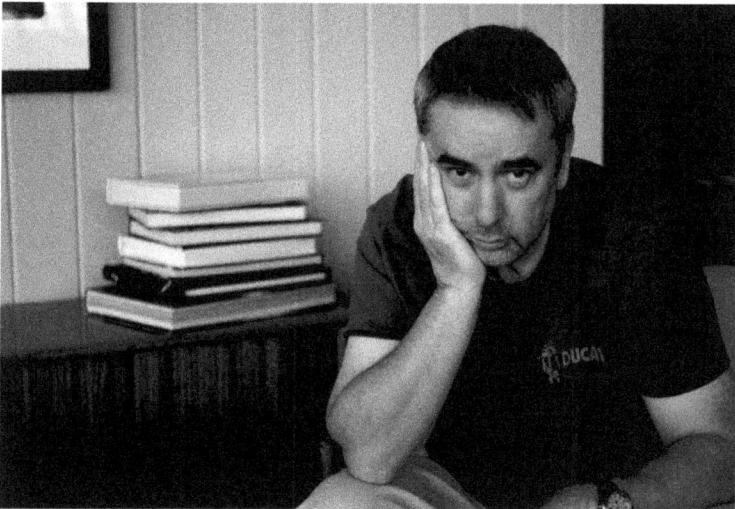

Photo Credit: Hannah Cowley Rath

Markus Innocenti tries not think too much about the sad fact that Orson Welles spent 95% of his professional life trying to fund films and only 5% actually making them. He's directed four feature films, a documentary or two, a handful of commercials and some music videos.
His first screenplay was produced. Which was nice.

AUTHOR LINKS & FREE DOWNLOADS

https://www.markusinnocenti.com/

Free downloads of material discussed in the books, along with full-color versions of images featured, can be accessed on my website.
Navigate to; Series>The Filmmaker's Art>Media

http://reddoglogic.tumblr.com/

Further pics and info can be found on the Red Dog Logic Tumbler blog.

THE FILMMAKER'S ART SERIES

Currently Available...

Vol 1. DECODING THE SCRIPT
Directors read scripts in ways that others don't, but the Clues are there for everyone to see once they understand how to 'decode'.

Vol 2. SELECTING FOR SUCCESS
Failure to properly prepare for production leads to bad choices and bad films — and sometimes good intentions have unfortunate results.

Vol 3. SHOOTING THE LIST
The Shot List is the Director's roadmap. This book discusses why it is important to have a List, and how to construct one.

Future Volumes... (Titles and Content Not Contractual)

Vol 4. EYE OF A POET
Working with a Director of Photography, understanding basics of Composition, Lighting and Lenses, and the use of Motion and Movement.

Vol 5. ACTORS ON SET
A deep dive into the challenges and rewards of the collaboration between Actors and Directors.

Vol 6. CUTTING FOR KEEPS
Delivering the movie you wanted to make.

Vol 7. MERCHANTS IN THE HOUSE OF FILM
An insider's look at the industry and the career path you might take.

www.ingramcontent.com/pod-product-compliance
Lightning Source LLC
Chambersburg PA
CBHW061732020426
42331CB00006B/1205